explore & discover
THE OUTER HEBRIDES

A PHOTO-LOCATION AND VISITOR GUIDEBOOK

VISIT THE MOST BEAUTIFUL PLACES, TAKE THE BEST PHOTOS

CHRISTOPHER SWAN

explore & discover
THE OUTER HEBRIDES
CHRISTOPHER SWAN

Copyright © fotoVUE Limited 2023.
Text and Photography: Copyright © Christopher Swan 2023.
Foreword Copyright © Julie Fowlis 2023.

Christopher Swan has asserted his right under the Copyright, Designs and Patents Act 1988 to be identified as the author of this work.

All rights reserved. No part of this book may be reproduced or transmitted in any form or by any means, electronic or mechanical, including photocopying, recording, or by any information storage and retrieval system without the written permission of the publisher, except for the use of brief quotations in a book review.

TRADEMARKS: fotoVUE and the fotoVUE wordmark are the registered trademarks of fotoVUE Ltd.

Publisher: Mick Ryan – *fotoVUE Ltd*.
fotoVUE Scotland Series Editor: Dougie Cunningham.
Additional research: Mick Ryan and Martyna Krol.
Design and layout by Ryder Design – www.ryderdesign.studio

All maps within this publication were produced by Don Williams of Bute Cartographics.
Map location overlay and graphics by Mick Ryan. Maps contain Ordnance Survey data
© Crown copyright and database right 2016.

A CIP catalogue record for this book is available from the British Library.

ISBN 978-1-7395083-2-6
10 9 8 7 6 5 4 3 2 1

The author, publisher and others involved in the design and publication of this guide book accept no responsibility for any loss or damage users may suffer as a result of using this book. Users of this book are responsible for their own safety and use the information herein at their own risk. Users should always be aware of weather forecasts, conditions, time of day and their own ability before venturing out.

Front cover: Tràigh Mheilein and the barren hills of Lewis. Fujifilm X–T2, 18–55mm f/2.8–f/4, ISO 200, 1/105s at f/11. Jul.
Rear cover left: The silhouettes of the Calanais stones at dawn. Fujifilm X–T2, 18–55mm f/2.8–f/4, ISO 200, 2s at f/5. Sep.
Rear cover right: A gannet flies past Stac Lee off the coast of Boreray. Fujifilm X–T2, 18–55mm f/2.8–f/4, ISO 200, 1/850s at f/5. Aug.
Opposite: The Seilebost viewpoint over to Luskentyre. Fujifilm X–T2, 10–24mm f/4, ISO 200, 1/750s at f/8. Oct.

Printed and bound in China by Latitude Press Ltd.

The west is the best.

**The End,
Jim Morrison**

CONTENTS

Index map	6
Detail map and locations	8
Acknowledgements	10
Foreword by Julie Fowlis	12
Introduction	14
Using this guidebook and getting the best image	16
Camera, lenses and captions	18
Access and behaviour	20
Getting to and around the Outer Hebrides	22
Where to stay, eat and get provisions	26
Gàidhlig / Gaelic	28
The Outer Hebrides weather and seasonal highlights	30
Outer Hebrides climate	32
The Northern Lights (Aurora Borealis) and the dark skies of the Hebrides	34
Outer Hebrides wildlife	38
Machair and seaweed	44
Classic Outer Hebrides locations	46

OUTER HEBRIDES NORTH: LEWIS AND HARRIS
AREA MAP 51

LEWIS introduction 54
1. Tolsta and Garry 56
2. The Northernmost Point 62
3. Dail Mòr, Dail Beag and Stac a' Phris 68
4. Village and Broch 74
5. Callanish 78
6. Great Bernera 86
7. The Bhaltos Peninsula 92
8. Uig 96
9. Mangersta 102

HARRIS
HARRIS introduction 112

AREA MAP 115
1. Luskentyre 116
2. Seilebost and Nisabost 130
3. Tràigh Iar and Macleod's Stone 142
4. Borve to Scarasta 148
5. Northton and Ceapabhal 156
6. Rodel and the Golden Road 164
7. North Harris 170
8. Scalpay 176

OUTER HEBRIDES SOUTH
AREA MAP 183

BERNERAY introduction 186
1 Tràigh Iar (West Beach) 188
2 East Beach 192

NORTH UIST introduction 196
1 The Northern Coast 200
2 The Atlantic Edge 206

BENBECULA introduction 220
1 Ruabhal 222
2 Culla 226

SOUTH UIST introduction 230
1 The beaches 232
2 Lochs and mountains 240

ERISKAY introduction 246
1 Prince Charlies Beach 248
2 The village 250

OUTER HEBRIDES FAR SOUTH
AREA MAP 256

BARRA introduction 258
1 Castlebay and Heabhal 260
2 The West Coast 264
3 North Barra 270
4 The East coast 278

VATERSAY introduction 284
1 The Gables 286
2 The beaches 288
3 Bàgh Bhatarsaigh 291
4 Traigh Siar 291
5 Bàgh a' Deas 292
6 Eòrasdail 294

ST KILDA
ST KILDA introduction 298

AREA MAP 301
1 Approach from the sea 302
2 Village bay 304
3 Main Street 306
4 The Gap and Conachair 310
5 Dùn and Ruabhal 312

About the Author 314
About fotoVUE 316
Location Index 318

Gannets circle Stac Lee off the coast of Boreray. Fujifilm X–T2, 18–55mm f/2.8–f/4, ISO 200, 1/2900s at f/5. Aug.

DETAILED MAP AND LOCATIONS

OUTER HEBRIDES NORTH: LEWIS AND HARRIS

LEWIS **54**
1. Tolsta and Garry 56
2. The Northernmost Point 62
3. Dail Mòr, Dail Beag and Stac a' Phris 68
4. Village and Broch 74
5. Callanish 78
6. Great Bernera 86
7. The Bhaltos Peninsula 92
8. Uig 96
9. Mangersta 102

HARRIS
1. Luskentyre 116
2. Seilebost and Nisabost 130
3. Tràigh Iar and Macleod's Stone 142
4. Borve to Scarasta 148
5. Northton and Ceapabhal 156
6. Rodel and the Golden Road 164
7. North Harris 170
8. Scalpay 176

OUTER HEBRIDES SOUTH

BERNERAY **186**
1. Tràigh Iar (West Beach) 188
2. East Beach 192

NORTH UIST **196**
1. The Northern Coast 200
2. The Atlantic Edge 206

BENBECULA **220**
1. Ruabhal 222
2. Culla 226

SOUTH UIST **230**
1. The beaches 232
2. Lochs and mountains 240

ERISKAY **246**
1. Prince Charlies Beach 248
2. The village 250

OUTER HEBRIDES FAR SOUTH

BARRA **258**
1. Castlebay and Heabhal 260
2. The West Coast 264
3. North Barra 270
4. The East coast 278

VATERSAY **284**
1. The Gables 286
2. The beaches 288
3. Bàgh Bhatarsaigh 291
4. Traigh Siar 291
5. Bàgh a' Deas 292
6. Eòrasdail 294

ST KILDA
1. Approach from the sea 302
2. Village bay 304
3. Main Street 306
4. The Gap and Conachair 310
5. Dùn and Ruabhal 312

ACKNOWLEDGEMENTS

Firstly, I'd like to thank Mick and Dougie at fotoVue for giving me the opportunity to visit, explore and photograph so many incredible Hebridean Islands. From the moment we discussed the project over a curry in Glasgow I have been so excited about it and it has been a huge part of my life for the past 5 years. There have been many challenges over the course of it: undertaking all the trips, the unpredictability of the weather, a pandemic and subsequent lockdowns, making the images and writing the book itself, but it really has been a dream commission. Thanks to Don for the brilliant maps and Nathan for both the excellent layout and putting up with my constant image changes.

To Joanne, my partner, thank you for being there with me on so many of these trips. For your love and encouragement, for always believing in me. Thank you for the endurance you've shown in waiting *"just another 10…20…30 minutes for the light"* as the rain beats down, and for spending all your holidays in the Hebrides with me.

To Mum, Dad, Stewart and Jenna, thank you for all your love and support. It has been amazing to spend time with you in many of these places. Thanks to Dad who not only taught me the basics of how to use a camera, but how to see and compose an image; without you this book wouldn't have happened. Thank you to Andy Hall for the inspiration and encouragement over the years.

To my best friend Nick. Sorry for chucking your anchor off the boat when it wasn't tied on. It's somewhere off the coast of Jura if anyone finds it.

To everyone who has shown an interest in the project, who has either commented on social media or asked about my trips, thank you, it has meant so much to me. Writing this book has been a long process and the encouragement from friends and family has been so important to me, particularly during lockdown when I could no longer visit the islands and these wonderful places seemed so far away.

Lastly, I'd like to thank the islands, which mean so much to me. There is a beautiful word in the Gaelic language which is *'cianalas'*. It doesn't directly translate into English but roughly equates to 'a homesickness or a longing for a place' and is what a Gael feels when they are far from home. These islands aren't my home (yet), but I do feel a yearning for them when I'm not there and after your visit, I'm sure you will too.

Christopher Swan
September 2023

Snow on the dunes at Luskentyre. Fujifilm X–T2, 18–55mm f/2.8–f/4, ISO 200, 1/20s at f/8. Feb.

FOREWORD BY JULIE FOWLIS

"Light is to photography what words are to poetry. It is the essential element, the heart and soul, the very essence of the art."
– George Eastman

The Outer Hebrides have long since been a source of inspiration for artists and creatives. Visual artists seek that very special light in the west, for which Gaelic has so many beautiful words – lainnir, aiteal, soillse, caimean. The colours of an t-Òg- Mhios (the young month, June) offer a gentle and luminous painterly light which colour island skies until the sun's brief disappearance into the Atlantic horizon. Conversely, in an Dùbhlachd (the dark month, December), nights are long and we actively seek that light in the short days.

This photographic collection serves to illuminate these places that are so dear; where the songs, stories and history are woven into our knowing of them and the infinite fine detail of place names hold fast to the ancient rocks which those living on Europe's western edge call home.

The captivating combination of ever changing light, crystal clear waters, dramatic weather, white shell-sand beaches and rocky coastlines make the Hebrides a stunning, and sometimes challenging, place to photograph.

The grace of the light in these lands, under an ever-changing expanse of sky, are captured beautifully by Chris in this book. The word for 'photograph' in Gaelic is 'dealbh' – but the word means more than simply a photo or an image. It implies the act of creating, crafting or shaping something, an artistic process. The made image references the craft, the care that is so clear to see in Chris's images.

Let the visuals in this book invite you in, to explore the islands, to experience our culture and language, and to be curious about the unique and stunning landscapes within these pages.

Julie Fowlis
September 2023

Portrait photo © Craig Mackay, Pictii.

'If snow could sing, it would sing like Julie Fowlis…'
– Robert Macfarlane

Julie Fowlis, born on North Uist and now based in the Highlands of Scotland, is an award-winning Scottish folk singer and musician, widely known for singing the theme songs to the Disney/Pixar animated film Brave, set in the Scottish Highlands. She grew up with music at home in the Outer Hebrides and with of course Scottish Gaelic which she often sings in, as well as the traditional mouth music/ *puirt a beul*. Her album 'alterum' is one of the best examples of her work, on which she sings many traditional Hebridean songs. She plays the whistle, pipes, accordion, melodeon, flute, oboe and cor anglais. She was Scotland's inaugural 'Tosgaire na Gàidhlig' (National Gaelic Ambassador) as well as the voice of Scottish Gaelic for the United Nations Declaration of Human Rights Project. Julie has won numerous awards including BBC Radio's Folk Singer of the Year. As well as touring solo and with collaborators, she is also a presenter for the BBC, Sky Arts and TG4.

You can buy Julie's music and find out about her forthcoming performances at *www.juliefowlis.com*

A summer day at Seilebost. Fujifilm X-T2, 18–55mm f/2.8–f/4, ISO 200, 1/160s at f/8. Jun.

INTRODUCTION

To the west of the Inner Hebrides are the Outer Hebrides (or Western Isles), *Na h-Eileanan Siar*, stretching for over 135 miles along the Atlantic edge of Scotland from the Butt of Lewis to Barra Head.

In the north is Lewis, the largest and most populous island with its bustling capital Stornoway. Lewis is home to the stone circle at Calanais, an incredible megalithic site of international importance for its historical, archaeological, and cultural value. The coastline of Lewis is rugged and dramatic, with towering cliffs and wave-lashed sandy beaches where Lewisian gneiss, one of the oldest rocks on earth, sparkles on the shorelines like the sea which eventually smooths it. Along the coast are the main crofting settlements, tight-knit communities situated between the sea and the vast area of moorland and peat bogs.

Joined to Lewis but separated by loch and mountains is Harris. An island of stunning natural beauty with white sandy beaches and turquoise seas contrasting with the barren rocky interior. It is a landscape which is simply breathtaking. Famed for Harris Tweed, this hand-woven woollen fabric is deeply tied to the culture and history of the Outer Hebrides and imbued with an essence of the land with the colours, patterns and textures of the natural environment revealing themselves in the fabric. Harris is an island which makes a profound impression on all who visit and the memory stays long after you make the crossing back to the mainland.

Across the scattered isles and skerries of the Sound of Harris is Berneray with its famous Tràigh Iar, the archetypical Hebridean beach with towering dunes, swaying marram grass and crashing waves. South over a causeway is North Uist home to ancient monuments, shapely hills and yet more beautiful sandy beaches where St Kilda can occasionally be glimpsed, tantalisingly out of reach on the western horizon. Benbecula sits between the Uists, an island where seawater, freshwater and land interplay and innumerable lochans glint amongst the moorland. To the south is the mountainous South Uist, its western coast lined by the machair, a colourful wildflower landscape created by windblown shell sand and encouraged by traditional farming practices. Then there is Eriskay, famed for Whisky Galore, Bonnie Prince Charlie and the eponymous breed of ponies.

Over the water is Barra, known as the Hebrides in miniature with a hilly interior and glorious sandy coast, famous for having the only airport with scheduled flights which uses a beach as a runway. Connected to Barra by a causeway is the island of Vatersay, home of the Raiders, crofters who when evicted by an absentee landowner returned to seize the land for themselves and their community.

Forty miles out in the Atlantic is the St Kilda archipelago, a vast volcanic caldera gradually sinking beneath the waves and a double UNESCO World Heritage Site due to its exceptional natural and cultural significance. St. Kilda's natural environment is extraordinary, not only is it visually dramatic with towering sea cliffs it also has the largest colony of northern gannets in the world. St. Kilda also holds immense cultural and historical value, the main island Hirta was inhabited for thousands of years by a small community that developed its own way of life in the challenging conditions before extreme hardship and isolation drove them from their homes in 1930.

These islands are the heartland of the Gaelic language once spoken throughout Scotland and Gaelic represents a cultural and ancestral identity that is deeply intertwined with the land, history, and way of life. It is a cornerstone of the islands' cultural identity and heritage. Despite the challenges it has faced over the years, Gaelic continues to play a vital role in the unique character of the Outer Hebrides and creates a sense of pride and connection amongst its residents.

The islands of the Outer Hebrides are special places which will leave a lasting impression on you. From the beauty of the landscape, to the ancient history and vibrant culture, to the warm and welcoming people the Outer Hebrides are islands which are to be treasured and appreciated.

Christopher Swan
September 2023

Tràigh Iar. Fujifilm X–T1, 14mm f/2.8, ISO 200, 0.7s at f/11. Apr.

USING THIS GUIDEBOOK TO GET THE BEST IMAGES

fotoVUE Explore & Discover photo-location and visitor guidebooks give you the information and inspiration to get to beautiful locations and take the best photographs.

In the right place

Each location chapter has a grey box titled 'How to get here' where there are written directions to the location along with four co-ordinates to the nearest car park or lay-by, including a scannable location QR-code. On the maps are location and sometimes viewpoint pins, and parking symbols.

Viewpoint 1
- **P** Lat/Long: 58.361340, -6.2165911
- **P** what3words: ///factories.outwit.handicaps
- **P** Grid Ref: NB534491
- **P** Postcode: HS2 0NN

The QR-code

Using your smart phone camera point the lens at the QR-code and your camera will scan the code that contains the parking location information as a lat-long co-ordinate. On some older phone operating systems you may have to have a QR-code reader app. Once read, your browser will open in Google maps and you can get directions from where you are to the parking spot of your chosen location.

///What3Words
Download the free app at *what3words.com*

Postcodes are great if you are going to a specific building but not ideal for getting to the middle-of-nowhere. Latitude/longitude is precise but it is a hassle to type 16-digits into a navigation app or sat-nav. Better is *what3words*, which assigns each 3m square in the world a unique three-word address that will never change. Download the free *what3words* app then either say, type or scan in the *what3words* of a location, click on navigate, open a map app and you will get directions to the location. You can save locations on your phone, which is useful if you plan on visiting several locations in a day or are on a trip; you can save them all before you set off. The *what3words* app can also take photographs and stamp the *what3words* location on your image as a useful reference source for where your images were taken. In the UK most emergency services use *what3words* so if you get into trouble whilst exploring in a remote location, use the app to help 999 know exactly where to find you.

Ordnance Survey maps

The relevant OS Explorer map (1:25 000) for each location is given at the beginning of each location section next to the introduction. There are several apps that allow you to download the relevant OS maps in return for a subscription. However, it is not recommended to rely solely on a mobile phone or tablet for navigation as batteries can run out and wireless connections can be lost.

Before you set off, study a map so that you know where you are going and give yourself plenty of time to get to your destination. Also, read the accessibility notes to check the distances and terrain to a location's viewpoints.

The fotoVUE maps

Our maps are created by the talented Don Williams of Bute Cartography, then an overlay is added with location and viewpoint pins along with points of interest and services.

Our map symbols

Our maps are detailed but with few symbols. The symbols that are important are:

A location chapter

A location chapter is marked by a numbered circle or pin and its name.

A location viewpoint

A viewpoint is marked by a small circle sometimes with the name of the viewpoint by it, or a reference to a viewpoint in the text such as VP1, VP2, V3 etc.

Footpaths - - - - - - - - - - - - - - -

Not all footpaths are marked on our maps, only footpaths that are useful to get to a location and its viewpoints.

Walking man symbol

Paths with a walking man represent longer walks of a few miles, often involving steep uphill walking. These may require navigation and use of map and compass. Sometimes we use them to clarify a right of way.

TRAVEL: ROADS

 Main A road
 B road
 Drivable track or minor road
 Fuel/EV charging
 Parking
 Ferry
 Harbour or Port
 Airport

FACILITIES

 Restuarant
 Cafe
 Bar/pub
 Whisky Distillerly
 Other Distillerly
 Grocery shopping/supermarket
 Souvenir shopping
 Vibrant nightlife
 Church
 Visitor centre/information
 Botanical gardens
 Museum
 Bus terminus
 Public toilets/restroom
 Hospital/medical centre
Swimming pool
Golf Course

TRAVEL: OFF ROAD

 Footpath/trail with hiker
 River crossing on foot
 National Trail
 Long bike packing routes

PROTECTED AREA

 National Park or Nature Reserve
National Trust for Scotland
UNESCO World Heritage site / area

LOCATIONS

 Location name, number & viewpoints
VP1: Beach
VP2: Rocks

NATURAL & CULTURAL FEATURES

 Waterfall
 Graveyard
 Castle
 Estate/Historic House
Point of cultural interest
 Shipwreck
 Lighthouse
 Peak name & elevation
Beinn Bheigeir △ 491m
 Wild swimming spot
 Surfing spot

ACCOMMODATION

 Hotel/chalets/glamping
 Hostel/highland dorm
 Bothy
 Campsite
 Motorhome/van & camp site
Parking for campervans

WILDLIFE

 Good red deer habitat
Dolphins seen here
 Seal watching spot
 Whale watching spot
 Coastal bird watching
 Puffins common here
Inland bird watching spot
Corn crake habitat
 Eagles common
 Mountain hare habitat
Otters seen here
 Wild goats
Highland coos

MAP KEY

At the right time

Each location in this book is accompanied by detailed notes on the optimum time of year and day to visit a location to get the best photographic results. Good light can occur at any time, however. Often the best time to visit a location is when conditions are rapidly changing, such as after a storm.

Weather

Check the weather forecast a few days before and the day before a planned outing. Recommended apps are *metoffice.gov.uk* and *yr.no*

Sun

Topography, sun position and weather determine how light falls on the land. Use the sun position compass on the front flap of this guidebook for sunrise and sunset times, to find out where the sun rises and sets on the compass (there is a big difference between summer and winter) and sun elevation (how high the sun rises in the sky).

Useful websites and apps include **The Photographer's Ephemeris** (*photoephemeris.com*), **photopills** (*photopills.com*) and *suncalc.org*

Exploration

This guidebook will help get you to some of the best photographic locations and viewpoints in the Hebrides. It is by no means exhaustive; use it as a springboard to discover your own viewpoints. Study a map to look for locations or just follow your instinct to discover your own.

CAMERA, LENSES AND CAPTIONS

Aesthetically, my approach to photography is always to strive for strong, graphic compositions with a desire to simplify the scene into its base elements. I grew up using film and like to get it right in-camera, minimising the amount of time I spend processing images. I do enjoy using long exposures, mainly to simplify water and skies, and create an ethereal atmosphere but aside from long exposures my images are intended to convey a realistic but artistic impression of the landscape.

Equipment list

Camera bodies
- Fujifilm X-E3
- Fujifilm X-T1
- Fujifilm X-T2
- Fujifilm X-100S

Lenses
- Fujinon XF 10–24mm f/4
- Fujinon XF 18–55mm f/2.8-f/4
- Fujinon XF 55–200
- Fujinon XF 35mm f/1.4
- Fujinon XF 14mm f/2.8

Filters
- Lee Seven 5 Filter System

Tripods
- Gitzo Mountaineer Tripod
- Manfrotto Magnesium Head

Opposite top: Chris and Alfie at Callanish, iPhone SE, Sep.
Bottom: Photographing Luskentyre from the kitchen window, iPhone SE, Jan.

Photo captions

The photo captions in fotoVUE guidebooks are in two parts:

1 Descriptive caption
First is a caption that describes where the photograph was taken, mentioning any references to viewpoints (e.g. VP1) in the accompanying text and any other useful information.

2 Photographic information
The second part of the caption lists the camera, lens, exposure, and the month the photograph was taken. This information is from the Exchangeable Image File Format (EXIF data) that is recorded on each image file when you take a photograph.

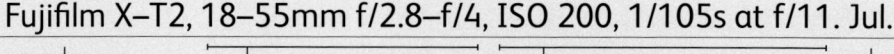

Fujifilm X–T2, 18–55mm f/2.8–f/4, ISO 200, 1/105s at f/11. Jul.

Make and model of camera | **Lens focal length** | **Light–Exposure information** The ISO setting, shutter speed and aperture that the photograph was taken at. | **The month taken** The month included in the caption enables you to know the (possible) type of weather and state of vegetation at the location.

ACCESS AND BEHAVIOUR

Being outdoors means living life to the full and should be enjoyed by all, but we have to share it with others and stay safe. Here is some information and guidelines on accessing the outdoors and looking after yourself.

The Scottish Outdoor Access Code

The Scottish Outdoor Access Code provides detailed guidance on the exercise of the ancient tradition of universal access to land in Scotland, which was formally codified by the Land Reform (Scotland) Act 2003. Under Scots law everyone has the right to be on most land and inland water for recreation, education and going from place to place providing they act responsibly. The basis of access rights in Scotland is one of shared responsibilities, in that those exercising such rights have to act responsibly, whilst landowners and managers have a reciprocal responsibility to respect the interests of those who exercise their rights. The code provides detailed guidance on these responsibilities. From: www.outdooraccess-scotland.scot

Be a respectful photographer

The obvious is always worth stating: do not climb over walls or fences, shut all gates, don't drop litter, pick up litter others have dropped, keep dogs at home or on a lead, drive slowly in rural and urban areas, give way to cyclists, agricultural vehicles and horse riders, park considerately, don't scare livestock and keep quiet (don't play music or fly drones near others) but always say hello to fellow outdoor enthusiasts. In short, follow the **the Scottish Outdoor Access Code**.

Respect other people

- Consider the local community and other people enjoying the outdoors
- Park carefully so access to gateways and driveways is kept clear
- Leave gates and property as you find them
- Follow paths but give way to others where it's narrow

Protect the natural environment
- Leave no trace of your visit; take all your litter home
- Don't have barbecues or fires
- Keep dogs under effective control
- Bag, and bin, dog poo

Enjoy the outdoors
- Plan ahead, check what facilities are open, be prepared
- Follow advice and local signs, and obey any social distancing measures

Busy viewpoints
As photography becomes more popular, some accessible locations and viewpoints can become busy in times of good light. In some circumstances this can cause conflict between photographers as they look for the best spot from which to compose their shot. If you arrive at a location and someone is already set up, give them space and don't get in their way. Talking and negotiating helps; they may be OK with you setting up next to them, or with you using their spot after they have finished. There are usually alternative viewpoints, but just make sure you aren't in their line of fire. If there is a crowd at a particular spot, it's often best just to find another viewpoint.

Mobility ♿
If you can't walk far or up steep slopes, or if you use a wheelchair or have an injury and need to know whether a location is suitable for you, each location chapter has a brief Access Notes section describing the terrain and distance from the road to a viewpoint. Most locations in this guidebook are usually not far from the road and some are roadside.

If a location or viewpoint has the wheelchair symbol, part or all of it will be accessible by wheelchairs. Bear in mind that access for wheelchair users may not be exactly as described in the text, and you should use your own judgment as to how far you proceed at any given location. And don't forget, driving around the countryside will present many superb photographic opportunities; just be careful where you stop – avoid stopping in passing places for more than a quick shot and always be aware of traffic.

Coastal locations
If you or others are in trouble call 999 and ask for the Coastguard. If you don't have a mobile phone, shout for help. Many locations in this guidebook are by the sea, on beaches and on rocky shorelines including cliff edges.

Before you go
- Wear appropriate clothing and footwear.
- Let someone know where you are going and at what time you plan to return.
- Take a fully charged mobile phone with you.
- Check the tide timetables so that you know when high and low tides will be.

Once outside
- Take extra care on rocky beaches that are often slippery and sharp.
- Stay away from cliff edges, especially if it's windy or if the ground is wet.
- Avoid walking below cliffs as many are unstable.
- Obey warning signs and don't climb over fences.
- If you get stuck in mud or quicksand, spread your weight, avoid moving and call for help.
- Always take a head torch with you for night photography.
- If you're taking a selfie, be safe.

GETTING TO AND AROUND THE OUTER HEBRIDES

Getting to the Hebrides is all part of the fun. Whether you are sailing across on the ferry or flying in a small plane you will get a great perspective of the islands on your journey. There is also the potential for photography, particularly on the ferries, with both regular sightings of whales and dolphins and also the distinctive views of the islands you get from being on the water. Whilst public transport is available in the Hebrides, travelling by car is the best way to ensure you get to the right place at the right time.

Ferry

Apart from Skye (which is connected to the mainland by the Skye Bridge) the most likely way you will arrive on a Hebridean island is by ferry. For me the boat over is always a delight, and whether it's a stormy day, or it's clear and calm; the journey across the water is always a symbolic one. Run by Caledonian Macbrayne (Calmac), their distinctive red, black and white boats have plied the waters of the Hebrides for over a century, an essential, lifeline service for the islanders bringing the majority of their supplies over from the mainland. They are increasingly popular and in the summer months booking is essential.

The ferry timetables are often co-ordinated with other public transport services both on the mainland and on the islands and there are connections to the rail network at Oban and at Mallaig see (www.scotrail.co.uk). If you are visiting more than one island, then Calmac provide discounted Hopscotch tickets for a number of island groups.

Check www.calmac.co.uk for full timetables and each islands introduction chapter in this book.

The main ports than ferries run from are Oban, Mallaig and Ullapool with several other small ports. You can also travel between some islands by ferry.

Air

There are number of airports in the Hebrides and with a journey time of an hour from Edinburgh or Glasgow of an hour this is an excellent way of making the most of your time. Car hire is available at the airports making a fly-drive trip a possibility but it is essential you book prior to travel. Viewing the Hebrides from the air and in particular flying to Barra, and landing on the only sand runway in the world might just be the highlight of your trip!

Loganair (www.loganair.co.uk) fly to and from Stornoway, Benbecula, Tiree, Barra and Islay.

Hebridean Air Services (www.hebrideanair.co.uk) fly from Oban to Coll, Tiree, Colonsay and Islay.

FERRIES FROM MAINLAND TO ISLANDS	Destinations	Duration	Car Ferry
PORT – calmac.co.uk			
Oban (PA34 4DB)	Castlebay, Barra	5hrs, 21m	Yes
	Lochboisdale, South Uist	5hrs, 42m	Yes
Mallaig (PH41 4QD)	Lochboisdale, South Uist	3hrs, 38m	Yes
Ullapool (IV26 2UR)	Stornoway, Lewis	2hrs, 45m	Yes
INTER ISLAND FERRIES			
Uig, Skye (IV51 9XX)	Lochmaddy, North Uist	1hr, 45m	Yes
	Tarbert, Harris	1hr, 40m	Yes
Barra	Eriksay	40m	Yes
North Uist, Berneray	Leverburgh, Harris	1h	Yes
FLIGHTS (Loganair – loganair.co.uk)			
Glasgow to Barra	–	1hr	–
Glasgow to Benbecula	–	1hr	–
Glasgow to Stornoway	–	1hr	–
Edinburgh to Stornoway	–	1hr	–
Inverness to Benbecula (via Stornoway)	–	1hr	–
Inverness to Stornoway	–	30m	–
Stornoway to Benbecula	–	30m	–

GETTING TO AND AROUND THE OUTER HEBRIDES

GETTING TO AND AROUND THE OUTER HEBRIDES

DISTANCES AND DRIVING TIMES TO MAIN PORTS			
	TAYINLOAN	**KENNACRAIG**	**OBAN**
Glasgow	113 miles (2hr 58m)	100 miles (2hrs, 42m)	90 miles (2hrs, 30m)
Edinburgh	161 miles (3hrs, 45m)	148 miles (3hrs, 30m)	122 miles (2hrs, 59m)
Carlisle, England-Scotland Border	212 miles (4hrs, 4m)	198 miles (3hrs, 47m)	189 miles (3hrs, 38m)
London	516 miles (9hrs, 45m)	503 miles (9hrs, 29m)	494 miles (9hrs, 16m)

Bus
There are regular bus connections to all the ferry terminals on the mainland at Ullapool, Mallaig, Oban and Tayinloan. Tickets can booked at (*www.citylink.co.uk*). On the islands themselves there are number of local services, which may only be once daily or even more infrequent. With enough planning it is possible to get around by bus however you will be constrained somewhat but the timetable.

Car
Travelling by car is the easiest way to get around the Hebrides however visitors may initially be unfamiliar with single track roads with passing places. We drive on the left hand side of the road in the UK with distances on road signs measured in miles and speed limits shown as miles per hour (mph). Speed limits in built up areas are 30mph unless otherwise indicated. On dual carriageways and motorways (none of these in The Hebrides!) the speed limit is 70mph unless you are towing or driving a van when it is 60mph. Rural roads are 60mph or 50mph respectively. Drink driving laws are strict with the legal limit set at 50 mg of alcohol in 100ml of blood. Essentially this can mean the a single pint of lager can put you over the limit. If you are visiting distilleries, make sure you take your tasting dram with you Throughout The Hebrides you may come across animals in the road. Sheep and Cows wander freely and should be given time to get off the road. Deer are a menace on the road at dusk and dawn and will often cross the road when you least expect. Otters, rabbits, hares and even goats are to be seen wandering the roads.

Navigation
Phone reception can be patchy at best or at times non-existent in the Hebrides so downloading any maps you require for navigation prior to your visit is advisable. 3G and 4G signals are becoming more widespread throughout the islands but depends greatly on the network. See each islands 'fact file' in the island's introduction chapter in this book for more information.

LOCHALINE	ARISAIG	MALLAIG	UIG, SKYE	ULLAPOOL
126 miles (3hs, 36m)	138 miles (3hrs, 31m)	145 miles (3hrs, 39m)	225 miles (5hrs, 21m)	223 miles (4hrs, 12m)
156 miles (4hrs, 8m)	178 miles (3hrs, 58m)	185 miles (4hrs, 12m)	250 miles (5hrs, 41m)	211 miles (4hrs, 20m)
223 miles (4hrs, 49m)	235 miles (4hrs, 40m)	243 miles (4hrs, 50m)	322 miles (6hrs, 39m)	307 miles (5hrs, 21m)
536 miles (10hrs, 32m)	549 miles (10hrs, 26m)	556 miles (10hrs, 35m)	653 miles (12hrs, 9m)	615 miles (10hrs, 52m)

Single Track Roads

Once you venture off the main roads you will be travelling on what are known as single track roads. These roads are only wide enough for one vehicle at a time and have regular passing places which allow you to get passed vehicles coming in the opposite direction. Many roads are steep, windy and very narrow and for drivers who are unfamiliar with them can be a daunting experience. These roads require care, caution and concentration and will take longer to negotiate than the milage suggests.

There is an etiquette in driving single track roads which will make driving them a much more pleasant experience for you and for other road users. Passing places are marked with a diamond or circular white sign and indicate where the road widens. If the passing place is on the left hand side and a vehicle is approaching, pull into the left. If in the same circumstance, the passing place is on the right hand side, stop in the centre, allowing the approaching vehicle to pass you via the passing place. In short stop, on the left hand side. There are a few golden rules to follow:

- **Passing places are not for parking**. In popular areas, there is a problem with visitors parking in passing places. This is inconsiderate, blocks the road, annoys locals and can cause a problem for emergency services.
- **Passing places should be used to allow overtaking**. Check your mirrors often, if there is somebody behind, pull in to the next passing place and allow them to overtake.
- **Do not pull up onto the verge to allow a vehicle to pass**. This causes a lot damage to road verges and can lead to cars getting stuck. If you approach a vehicle and there are no passing places, one driver will have to reverse.
- **Take particular care** passing bikes and pedestrians on single track roads.
- Give way to vehicles coming uphill.
- If you are visiting The Hebrides in a campervan, motorhome or with a caravan it is vital that you are confident in reversing.
- Wave! Give a cheery wave if a driver has pulled in for you.

WHERE TO STAY, EAT AND GET PROVISIONS

Welcome. How are you?
Fàilte. Dè do chor?

There is no better source of information about where to stay, eat and buy provisions in the Outer Hebrides than the **Outer Hebrides Tourism** website: *www.visitouterhebrides.co.uk*, the **Visit Scotland** website: *www.visitscotland.com/places-to-go/islands/outer-hebrides* and the individual island websites. Most of these sources are kept up to date and you can book accommodation direct rather than through a third party. They are also a mine of information about what to do and island culture.

www.visitouterhebrides.co.uk (Outer Hebrides Tourism website). *www.visitscotland.com* (VisitScotland is Scotland's national tourist board).

Lewis	isle-of-lewis.com
Harris	explore-harris.com
Berneray	isleofberneray.com (community run website)
North Uist	isle-of-north-uist.co.uk
Benbecula	isle-of-benbecula.co.uk
South Uist	isle-of-south-uist.co.uk
Eriskay	isle-of-south-uist.co.uk/isle-of-eriskay
Barra	explore-isle-of-barra.co.uk • isleofbarra.com
Vatersay	visitouterhebrides.co.uk

Island fact files in this book

In addition, in the introduction to each island in this book is an island fact file which gives further information including whether vehicles are allowed, main towns, car and bike rental, public transport information, accommodation, festivals and events, eating out and provisions.

Support the islands: provisions and eating out

Buy provisions locally, grab a coffee and cake, a beer or dram, buy locally-made gifts and eat out when you can, (don't miss the locally caught and smoked fish, and venison if you are an omnivore) and you will be making a positive contribution to the economies of the island communities.

Visit *www.visitouterhebrides.co.uk* and download the following leaflets:

- Made in Outer Hebrides: a guide to the arts & crafts on the islands
- Eat Drink Hebrides
- Community Shops

Accommodation

There is a wide range of accommodation including hotels, hostels, B&Bs and self-catering cottages on the islands. Book accommodation early as places fill up fast.

As well as the previously mentioned Outer Hebrides websites, the following sites are also useful:

scottishcamping.com	hostelworld.com
hostel-scotland.co.uk	hostellingscotland.org.uk
lhhscotland.com	cottages.com
unique-cottages.co.uk	airbnb.co.uk

Wild camping

Wild camping is also permitted, but anyone wild camping should always follow the guidance given in the **Scottish Outdoor Access Code**.

The code defines wild camping as:

Lightweight, done in small numbers and only for two or three nights in any one place. You can camp in this way wherever access rights apply, but help to avoid causing problems for local people and land managers by not camping in enclosed fields of crops or farm animals and by keeping well away from buildings, roads or historic structures. Take extra care to avoid disturbing deer stalking or grouse shooting. If you wish to camp close to a house or building, seek the owner's permission.

Leave no trace by:
- taking away all your litter
- not causing any pollution
- removing all traces of your tent pitch and of any open fire. Wherever possible, use a stove rather than light an open fire. If you do wish to light an open fire, keep it small,

under control, and supervised – fires that get out of control can cause major damage, for which you might be liable. Never light an open fire during prolonged dry periods or in areas such as forests, woods, farmland or on peaty ground or near to buildings or in cultural heritage sites where damage can be easily caused. Heed all advice at times of high risk. Remove all traces of an open fire before you leave.

Campervan and motorhomes

Campervan and motorhomes have grown increasingly popular in recent years and are catered for very well across the islands. Please note that The Outdoor Access Code states that access rights do not apply to motor vehicles – **sleeping in a van is not wild camping.**

Plan ahead

Essential to download is the invaluable campervan leaflet from: *www.visitouterhebrides.co.uk* which has a detailed map showing:

- Campsites & aires, and overnight parking for self-contained motorcaravans only.
- Designated parking spots
- Laundrettes
- Household waste point
- Grocery shops & fuel stations
- Calor gas
- Recycling points
- Public toilets
- Chemical toilet disposal points

Outer Hebrides Tourism has leaflets that I recommend you download from: *www.visitouterhebrides.co.uk/planning-your-trip/leaflets*
These include:
- Bird of Prey Trail
- Sail Hebrides
- Eat Drink Hebrides
- Walking and Cycling Routes

WHERE TO STAY, EAT AND GET PROVISIONS

GÀIDHLIG / GAELIC

The Hebrides are the stronghold of the Gàidhlig language and culture. On your visit to the islands you may notice the language spoken in shops or pubs, you will hear it sung if you listen to traditional music and you will definitely see it written on road signs. Thought to have been spoken since the 4th Century, this Celtic language was once used widely across Scotland, with many place names able to trace their etymological roots to the Gaelic language. The language declined in use throughout much of Scotland, however it always remained in the Hebrides and along the western coast of the mainland.

Gaelic now is enjoying a resurgence. There is a Gaelic language TV station; BBC Alba. Gaelic schools are becoming more widespread throughout the country and the popularly of language-learning apps like Duolingo has brought Gaelic to a new audience, however it is in the Hebrides that you are more likely to come across it on a day to day basis. When visiting you can easily get by without knowing any Gaelic, after all, the vast majority of Gaelic speakers also speak English and the road signs are bi-lingual however learning some of the language will enrich your understanding of the landscape immeasurably and can even benefit your photography.

I believe an understanding of the landscape is fundamental to creating good landscape photography, and an excellent way to gain an understanding of the landscape is through the people who named it. No matter where you are in the world, the interaction between people and their landscape can reveal so much – I'm always amazed when studying maps at just how much of the landscape has been named, although it can be puzzling if you cannot understand the words! It is clear from reading maps today how important the landscape was to the Gaels of old, and we can definitely learn about the landscape from what features they chose to name.

Take for example the Gaelic word Dearg, meaning Red. If you see this applied to a mountain, it is a safe bet to assume that when the sun is low in the sky, the rocks will take on a bright red hue. Or the word Garbh, meaning 'rough or rugged'. This could be a particularly craggy hill with a bouldery slope which might offer some good foreground opportunities for a wider view, or its could just be a tricky walk! How about Darach or Daraich, meaning Oak? The chances are that if you encounter oakwood along the Atlantic coast you will find some interesting gnarled specimens worthy of investigation. On your journeys throughout Scotland you might encounter the place name Tarbert or Tarbet and notice that they are all positioned on a neck of land between two water bodies. This is from the Gaelic An Tairbeart, which essentially means "carry across" – it is a portage site for people to move boats from one water body to another!

The wealth of intrigue that opens up from just a basic grasp of landscape names can add so much to your enjoyment and understanding of the landscape, hopefully the list below sparks your intrigue. The following list gives a number of common Gaelic place names or landscape features which will aid your understanding of the landscape and if you would like to understand more, the book "Reading the Gaelic Landscape" by John Murray is a fantastic resource.

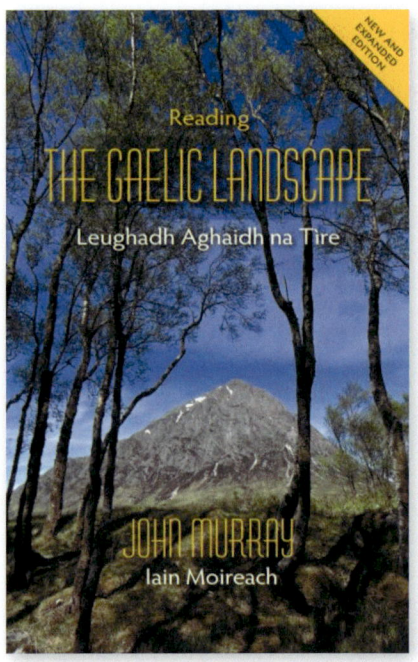

Gaelic	English
Abhainn	River
Achadh	Field
Àrd or **Aird**	High
Acarsaid	Anchorage
Aiseag	Ferry
Allt	Stream
Bàta	Boat
Bàn	White
Bealach	A mountain pass or col
Beag	Small or little
Beith	Birch
Beinn	Hill
Caol	Strait (Kyle)
Ceann	Head (Usually anglicised to Kin – for example Kinloch Rannoch is The Head of Loch Rannoch
Cnoc	Hillock
Bòidheach	Beautiful
Dearg	Red
Darach	Oak
Dubh	Black
Eas	Waterfall
Eagach	Jagged
Eilean	Island
Garbh	Rough or Rugged
Gorm	Blue blue/grey
Inbhir	Mouth of watercourse
Iolaire	Eagle
Làirig	Pass
Liath	Grey
Maol	Bald
Mhor or **Mór**	Large or great.
Òr	Gold
Ròn	Seal
Sneachda	Snow
Sròn	Nose shaped
Tiobar	Well
Tigh	House
Uaine	Green
Uisge	Water. As in Uisge beatha / Whisky (the water of life)

GÀIDHLIG / GAELIC

THE OUTER HEBRIDES WEATHER AND SEASONAL HIGHLIGHTS

"If you don't like the weather, then just wait 5 minutes"

It's a phrase which could easily have been written with the Hebrides in mind. The whims and vagaries of the weather on the islands off the west coast of Scotland are the stuff of legend and a source of constant discussion. The predominate prevailing wind in Scotland is from the west and the first land mass that wind hits is the Hebrides. It can therefore be windy and wet. That's not to say it's all cloud and rain, there are beautiful clear sunny days where the water is calm and you might brave the waters of the Atlantic for swim. But the days when the clouds scud over the land, with heavy downpours and occasional blasts of illumination? Those are the days when the Hebrides are absolutely magical. Get your jacket on, and get out there because that is when the best images are made.

SPRING – March, April, May

Spring is a fantastic time to visit the the Hebrides. As the land wakes up from its slumber, the days begin to lengthen and the quality of the light is almost as good as winter. It is not uncommon to have a long spell of settled clear weather in spring. There may still be snow on the higher hills, particular on sheltered north faces where it delicately traces out the lines of gullies and crags. The gorse begins to bloom in May and in the sheltered woodlands and on some coastal areas bluebells flourish. The yellow flag iris also brings a bright pop of yellow to marshy areas and the machair begins to bloom at the end of spring. Puffins and corncrakes return form their winter grounds in May and common dolphins start to be seen in the Atlantic. Unfortunately the end of spring brings about the start of the dreaded midge season.

SUMMER – June, July, August

Summer can be a frustrating time for photography in the Hebrides. Often the settled spring weather will give way to a *dreich* and damp summer with low cloud obscuring the hills. On sunny days, out of the golden hours, the light can be harsh and sometimes frustratingly hazy. On days like this, head to the beach, the sun on the turquoise sea is idyllic and once you're done with photography, make the most of the sun; it doesn't happen too often! Sitting at a latitude of 56 degrees north, the days are very long with sunrise at the summer solstice around 4:30 and sunset at 22:15. It therefore takes some dedication to make the most of the golden hour, however photographing a warm summer sunset in The Hebrides is a lovely experience. The heather comes into bloom in August and brings a beautiful

purple hue to the hills. The machair is at its best between July and August with species changing as the season progresses. The best areas of machair is in South Uist however, it can be found in many coastal locations in the Hebrides on the low-lying ground on the landward side of the dunes. It is an amazing sight, with a huge number of wild flower species creating carpet of colour buzzed by bees and insects. Of great interest to the macro photographer, studies of the machair can also be undertaken with great results on overcast days when the colours appear at their most saturated.

AUTUMN – September, October, November

Autumn is a great season in the Hebrides. Whilst not blessed with many areas of woodland to experience the changing colours, there are some areas to photograph this stunning yearly spectacle. The hills turn russet as the bracken dies back and the marram grass on the dunes begins to yellow, looking especially good in the slanting low sun at the now lengthening golden hours at both ends of the day. The nights draw in and on clear nights the milky way makes an appearance again after the twilight of summer nights. October is the rutting season and the roaring of stags may often be heard, Rum in particular has a huge population of deer at Kilmory Bay. The midge and tick season comes to a welcome end at the end of September.

WINTER – December, January, February

In winter the Hebrides can be a very wild place, but also incredibly photogenic. Atlantic storms lash the coast with huge waves breaking onto the shoreline making for some powerful images. Be very careful in these conditions, you will often be far from help. The hours of daylight are very short, sometimes only 7 hours long, but with the sun siting low in the sky you are blessed with a day-long Golden Hour.

Once the sun has set, the jet black skies, devoid of light pollution are perfect for astrophotography. The northern lights are often seen on clear nights in winter and it is worth subscribing to alerts from Glendale Aurora *www.glendaleskye.com/aurora-alerts-app.php* to make sure that you don't miss them. Whilst the colours are not as intense as the lights seen further north in Iceland or Canada, just seeing the lights is a magical experience. Whilst the Hebrides are at a northerly latitude, snowfall is not that common and the salt air tends to disperse it quickly from low lying areas. Skye occasionally gets a decent dump of snow and on those days the Cuillin take on an even more alpine appearance.

THE OUTER HEBRIDES CLIMATE

Whether it is sunny, or wet and windy, the Hebrides are always dramatic. The islands take the full force of westerly Atlantic storms and the Butt of Lewis has been recorded as being the UK's windiest spot, however in summer, due to the Gulf Stream, the Hebrides' sea temperatures can be as warm as Cornwall at the south-west tip of UK; great if you like swimming. It is because of the Gulf Stream, that brings warmer waters across the Atlantic from the south-east USA, that the Hebrides have a mild climate, despite their northerly latitude. Whilst inland, when the Highlands are snow-covered, the average winter temperature in the Hebrides is 6 °C (44 °F) and snow is rare on most westerly islands. Topography and land mass however also play a part and the high peaks, especially on Skye, are regularly snow covered, with the glens often filled with cold low-lying mist and fog.

The Outer Hebrides, generally, get slightly more sun and less rain than the Inner Hebrides, the latter getting more frosty days and snow. Average maximum temperatures are 12 °C (53 °F), average minimum is 6 °C (44 °F). May is the sunniest month, April to June the driest, December and January the wettest. Climate change and the movement of the jet stream have an influence and some years are seeing less rain and more sun, whilst it can be raining on the mainland, you won't need an umbrella in the Hebrides, some summers have seen only 10% of the average rainfall.

Weather can be localised, on one side of an island you may get rain, whilst on the other side there will be glorious sunshine.

Pack a jacket in summer, night temperatures drop quickly at sunset with the lowest temperatures just before sunrise. In high summer the days are long, and the nights short, making sunset late and sunrise very early (see the sun compass on the front flap for sunrise/sunset times and day length) and in June it never gets completely dark and in the depths of winter the sun stays low on the horizon all day in a perpetual golden hour (cloud cover dependent) for 6 or 7 hours.

"Azure. Turquoise. Cerulean. Aquamarine. I'm struggling to find enough words to describe the different shades of blue that I encounter on my travels across the length and breadth of Lewis and Harris in the Outer Hebrides."
Audrey Gillan

The Hebrides are renowned for their changeable weather (lots of rainbows and squalls) and celestial light, which when combined with the rich blues of the sky and the sea, make the Hebrides a visual delight at any time of year.

Met office weather station averages

Outer Hebrides: Stornoway, Lewis

Location: 58.214, -6.325
Altitude: 15m above mean sea

Inner Hebrides: Lusa, Skye

Location: 57.257, -5.809
Altitude: 18m above mean sea level

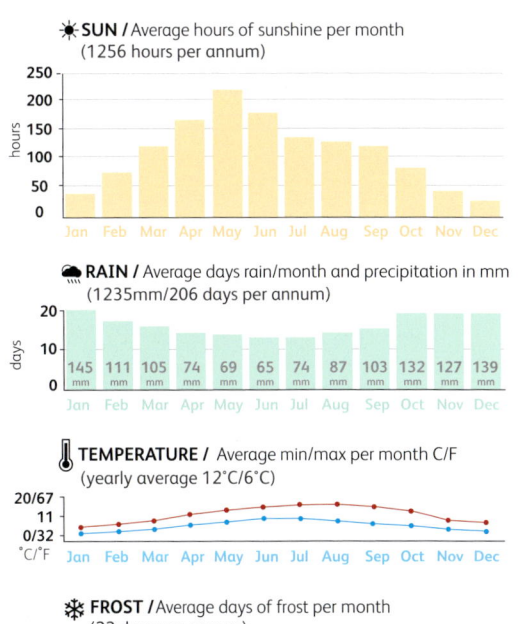
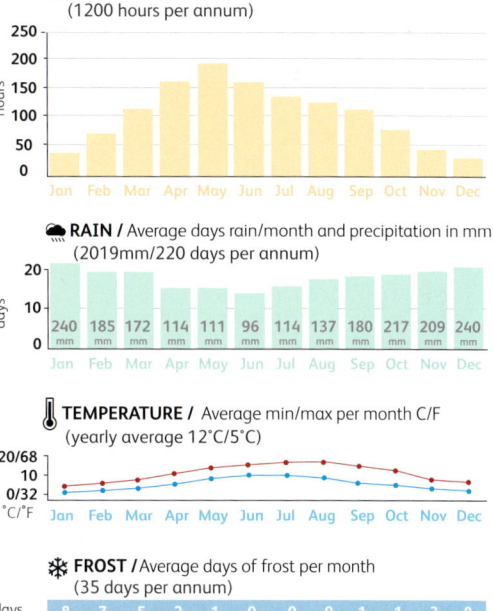

THE OUTER HEBRIDES CLIMATE   33

THE NORTHERN LIGHTS (AURORA BOREALIS)...

Graphic representation of the Bortle Scale.

Light Pollution

The Hebrides have excellent dark skies, generally unspoiled by light pollution unless you are near a large town. This means that not only are the Hebrides great for witnessing and photographing the Aurora Borealis but also the Milky Way, stars and planets. In the February edition of Sky and Telescope magazine an American amateur astronomer, John Bortle came up with a light pollution scale that rates the darkness of a site. Generally the Hebrides skies are very dark, from Bortle Class 1 to Bortle Class 3. In fact the island of Coll was designated a 'dark sky community' in 2013 by the International Dark Sky Association and the Isle of Gigha has created a non-profit community group, Dark Skies Gigha, which has been named as a Dark Sky Discovery Site by the UK Dark Sky Discovery Partnership.

In each islands' introduction fact file, its Bortle scale is listed.

Aurora Borealis (Na Fir Chlis 'The Nimble Men' in Scottish Gaelic folklore)

Caused by electrons from the sun exciting atoms and molecules in the Earth's atmosphere to subsequently release photons of light, the Aurora Borealis or northern lights are a magical phenomenon and can be seen in the Hebrides and the rest of Scotland. While the aurora is active all year it requires dark skies to see clearly, making the longer nights from autumn to spring the best time to view them. The best season generally extends from late August to mid-April. Avoid light polluted areas when taking Aurora Borealis images, and look for interesting foregrounds.

We are currently in period of high solar activity when the sun has the highest number of sunspots, solar flares and coronal mass ejections (CME) and, therefore is most active. When CMEs collide with Earth's magnetosphere they can cause geomagnetic storms and aurorae. So for the next few years (2024 onwards) you stand a good chance on a clear night of witnessing them.

KP Northern Lights forecast

Glendale Skye have produced an app which you can download from: *aurora-alerts.uk*

It is worth subscribing to get aurora alerts to make sure that you don't miss them.

One measurement of aurora activity is the KP index which has a range from 0–9, the higher the KP number the further south you can see the aurora and the more intense it will be. It's always worth going out for a look even if the KP index is low; also the forecast can change quickly, the KP can be high and it may not appear. However, cloud cover is your biggest enemy, clear skies are best.

KP 1–3: Quiet activity and feint, predominant colour is green.

KP 4–6: Very active, yellow, bluish, or purple tones. Possibility of ribbons, bands and pillars.

Aurora coronas are also possible.

KP 7–9: Strong aurora storms, very active. High chances of multiple colours including red.

A KP Index of 5 is common in the Hebrides, and some have witnessed spectacular Aurora coronas.

Photographing the Northern Lights

For DSLR and mirrorless cameras
- Bring a tripod and plenty of spare batteries.
- Aperture: f/1.4–f/3.5.
- Shutter Speed: Your shutter speed will be largely influenced by how fast the aurora is moving.

... AND THE DARK SKIES OF THE HEBRIDES

The Aurora Borealis at Clachan Shannda. Fujifilm X–T2, 14mm f/2.8, ISO 1000, 30s at f/2.8. Mar.

- 15–30 seconds for slow moving aurorae like arcs and diffuse glows.
- 5–15 seconds for bright dancing bands and pillars.
- 1–5 seconds for bright overhead coronas.
- ISO: 800–6400: use the ISO as the final control of the overall exposure.

If your image is too dark, increase the ISO (or vice versa).

- Focal Length: 14–24mm would be ideal.
- Focusing: use manual focus but don't twist your focus ring to the furthest left, or put the arrow in your viewfinder by the infinity symbol – as on most lenses this is not infinity. Better to manually focus on a bright star or planet or focus on a distant house/streetlight on the horizon. This will set your lens at infinity, some then use gaffer tape to fix it in position.

For smartphone cameras
- Make sure your battery is fully charged.
- Turn off all apps to save power.
- Attach your phone to a phone tripod in andscape orientation.

- Set your phone camera to manual mode or use a camera app (there are specialist aurora apps available) if it doesn't have a native manual camera app.
- Use the same settings as described above for a DSLR or Mirrorless camera.
- Some phones have native Night Modes, some that take multiple images and combine them, and some of these can be used handheld without the need for a tripod.

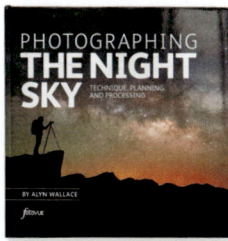

If you want to learn more about night sky photography, fotoVUE have published the definitive bible to night sky photography, *Photographing The Night Sky* by Alyn Wallace. You can buy a copy at fotovue.com and get 20% off by using the coupon code: COLL

In amongst the dunes at Reef. Fujifilm X-T2, 14mm f/2.8, ISO 200, 1/15s at f/11. Sep.

OUTER HEBRIDES WILDLIFE

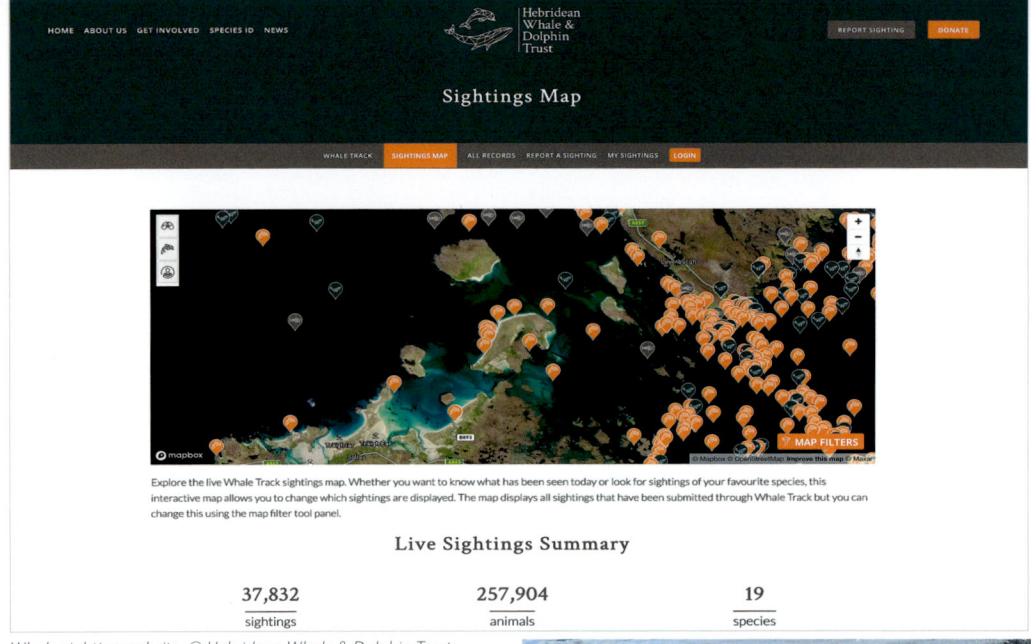

Whale sighting website. © Hebridean Whale & Dolphin Trust.

The Outer Hebrides' low population density, absence of intensive farming, island isolation, the varied habitats from sea and lochs to mountain top, and the influence of the Gulf Stream make it a haven for wildlife with a rich diversity of species — from sea eagles to seals the islands (and the seas around them) are packed with fascinating creatures. Some are easier to spot than others, sightings of red deer for example are commonplace but seeing (and not just hearing) a corncrake is a massive stoke of luck. In order to maximise your chances of being lucky, planning and fieldcraft are essential. For more information on learning these skills check out *Photographing Wildlife in the UK* (fotoVUE) by Andrew Marshall.

Here are some key species to look out for and where to find them. Binoculars are useful, as is a zoom lens.

Whale, dolphin, porpoise, basking sharks

The waters around the Hebrides teem with sea-life due to a combination of the Gulf Stream and its intersection with

Atlantic white sided dolphin. © Hollandvk.

the cold waters of the Atlantic creating the ideal conditions for the growth of plankton, the microscopic organism at the base of the food chain.

Patience, and luck is needed to spot whales, dolphin, and porpoise (collectively known as cetaceans). Twenty-three species have been recorded in Hebridean waters. There is an app and website, the **Whale Trail** – *whaletrail.org*, that will help you spot and identify these wonderful creatures.

Basking shark – Coll. © Martin Prochazkacz.

Otters. © Andrew Marshall.

Minke whale – Coll. © Katie HM.

Grey seal.

There is an interactive map that records recent sightings at the website which will help you locate cetaceans. Several species of dolphin and porpoise, including the harbour porpoise, Atlantic white-sided dolphin, bottlenose dolphin, orcas (killer whales) – present but rarely seen – and the humpback whale can be seen year-round in open and coastal waters. In summer look out for the common dolphin. The sea around the Butt of Lewis and down towards Tiumpan Head is recognised as an important area for the lesser-known Risso's dolphin. Minke whales and basking shark migrate into the Sea of the Hebrides during the summer and can be seen feeding at the surface between June and October each year. There are several boat trip operators, based on most of the islands, specialising in dolphin, shark and whale spotting.

Seals and otters

You stand a great chance of spotting seals and otters on the coast of the Outer Hebrides. Common and grey seals are often seen basking on the rocks and are frequently seen in and around harbours. Grey seals have their pups in October, please keep your distance. The European otter (they aren't sea otters) are common all around the coast, in saltwater lochs and inland freshwater, to spot them being stealth-like is important as otters are elusive and shy. Lookout for a bobbing head, a disappearing tail out to sea or a trail of bubbles, and if you do, be still and quiet and as always with wildlife spotting, let the subject come to you. Your best chance of seeing one is at dusk or dawn, particularly on an incoming tide when they feed. Their tracks are often seen in the sand. Hots spots for otters on the Isle of Lewis include the South Lochs and Uig and Bernera Districts, and the Southeast and Bays District of Harris.

OUTER HEBRIDES WILDLIFE

Puffins.

Puffins

These characterful little birds are an absolute delight and make their summer homes on a number of Hebridean islands. Completely unafraid of humans it is possible to get quite close to the birds, and photograph them in their natural habitat. Great places to see the puffins are on the offshore islands of St Kilda (home to 136,000 pairs of Atlantic puffins, about 30 percent of the UK total breeding population), the Shiants, Flannan Isles, Sula Sgier, Rona and Mingulay. Puffins arrive at the end of April and start to leave in August.

Great Skuas

Also known as Bonxies, these pirates of the skies are famous for dive-bombing unfortunate walkers. They can be found throughout the Hebrides in summer and are fierce scavenging birds who will often harass other smaller birds for food. If you are entering bonxie territory – beware!

Great Skua or a Bonxie.

St Kilda.

Pink-footed geese.

Gannet.

Birds – general

Three hundred and twenty seven species of birds have been recorded and more than 100 breed. Seabirds that inhabit the coastal areas of the islands include shag, northern gannets, northern fulmars, kittiwakes, guillemots and multiple species of gull. Oystercatchers and curlews are seen at the South Lochs between Loch Seaforth and Loch Erisort. Common eider and long-tailed duck are found in the shallow water around Lewis. Redshank, greenshank, ringed plover and dunlin. Shelduck and red-breasted merganser are to be seen on Loch Erisort, and large numbers of greylag geese and lapwing are found throughout the district. Pink-footed geese can be spotted on Lewis in the spring, along with greylag. Oystercatcher, ringed plover, bar-tailed godwit and dunlin are the most numerous species on the sand flats; the Atlantic beaches are particularly important to turnstones, purple sandpipers and sanderling. On the machair, oystercatcher, ringed plover, lapwing and dunlin are dominant.

OUTER HEBRIDES WILDLIFE

Birds of prey
Birds of prey in the Outer Hebrides include the spectacular golden eagles (90 pairs) and white-tailed eagle (aka. the sea eagle), hen harrier, merlin, short-eared owl and if you are lucky, peregrine falcons which nest on sea cliffs, Loch Stiapavat and Loch Sgioport are the most reliable locations. Most of these species can be seen across all the islands. With a wingspan of over 2 metres, the golden eagle is a true giant of the skies. Once you have seen one, you are unlikely to get it confused with the buzzard (AKA the tourist eagle) ever again. The white-tailed eagle or sea eagle was reintroduced to the Hebrides in 1975 after being hunted to extinction in the 1920s. Even larger than the golden eagle, there are 25 breeding pairs within the Outer Hebrides.

The good people at Visit Outer Hebrides and the RSPB have published a Birds of Prey Trail pamphlet which is invaluable, and highlights areas where birds pf prey are likely to be seen and also observatories and bird hides, such as the North Harris Eagle Observator and the Ravenspoint visitor centre overlooking Loch Erisport home to white-tailed eagles.

Corncrake
The corncrake is a shy and elusive bird known for its distinctive "crek crek" call. It returns to the Hebrides in April and makes its home in long grass and reeds within costal locations. Once a common bird, it is now only found in a few locations in Scotland. The Balranald RSPB reserve on North Uist is one of the best places to see corncrake.

Red Deer and other mammals
"Red deer are one of the symbols of Scotland, as much a visual shorthand for the Highlands and islands as the thistle." **The Scotsman**

Red deer are found on most islands and are usually at their most active around dusk and dawn. October sees the deer coming down from the higher hills for the rut, during which the males fight for the females — the best times to witness the rut is just after sunrise. The bellowing of stags echoing around the hills is an atmospheric indicator of autumn. Outer Hebrides red deer are thought to be genetically pure, meaning they haven't hybridised with sika deer. Research suggests that they were brought to the Outer Hebrides by Neolithic humans 4,500-5,500 years ago, although there is some dispute about this.

Highland Coo
Shaggy-haired, horned and with a lovely docile temperament, highland cows are found throughout the Hebrides and will usually stand still for long enough to take the classic postcard shot.

Little owl. © Andrew Marshall.

White-tailed eagle. © Andrew Marshall.

RSPB Bird of Prey leaflet.

Corncrake. © Gergosz.

Red deer.

Highland cows.

Border Collie

Crazy farm dogs who will occasionally follow you along the beach or up a hill. They are exceptionally clever animals and a vital member of the team when it comes to rounding up the wandering sheep at shearing time. Approach with caution, they will often want sticks throwing for hours.

Resources

Island websites:
- The Sea of Hebrides (see a story map at: www.storymaps.arcgis.com)
- www.whaletrail.org
- www.visitouterhebrides.co.uk/see-and-do/wildlife
- www.nature.scot
- www.rspb.org.uk

Nature Reserves

- Loch Stiapabhat Nature Reserve and Observatory, Isle of Lewis
- Loch Na Muilne Nature Reserve, Arnol, Isle of Lewis,
- Balranald RSPB Reserve, North Uist
- South Uist Nature Reserve
- Monach Islands Nature Reserve
- St Kilda World Heritage Site

MACHAIR

Unique to the west coast of Scotland and Ireland, Machair, a Gaelic word meaning fertile, low-lying grassy plain, is the flat or undulating carpet of wild flowers and grass found on west facing coastlines in the Hebrides. They are fascinating to visit and photograph, both the flora and birds, and are a perfect place to spot dolphins and seals. The machair was formed by calcerous shell fragments brought in by waves and then blown in by the wind, forming an alkaline soil low in nutrients, ideal for flowering plants, herbs and grasses. The machair is a semi-natural habitat, traditional Hebridean farming, tree clearance, low density grazing and the spreading of seaweed as natural fertiliser, aided its development into the beautiful and diverse carpet of plant species we see today. In the Hebrides there is a balance struck between food production and nature conservation.

Plant species include common meadow grass and red fescue, red clover, bird's-foot-trefoil, yarrow and daisies and rarer species such as lesser-butterfly orchid, Hebridean spotted orchid, marsh orchid and, on Coll and Barra, Irish lady's-tresses. You may spot iris, silverweed, ragged-Robin and poppies.

Kelp washes up on the machair, protecting it from erosion and as the kelp decays it provides food for insects which in turn are prey for wading birds and gulls. This habitat, because of its rich insect diversity, is also home to corn crake, twite, dunlin, common redshank, linnets, corn buntings and ringed plover and also several insect pollinators including several species of bumble bees.

Spring is the best time to visit for bird watching, with the machair in full bloom in June and to mid-August. The machair is under threat from rising sea levels and increasing storms which erodes it and also because of the decline of traditional farming and grazing.

Where to find machair

explore & discover THE OUTER HEBRIDES

The west coasts of:
The Uists	196, 230
Barra	258
Vatersay	284
Northton, Harris	156

explore & discover THE INNER HEBRIDES

Balevuiln on Tiree	212
West coast of Coll	200

SEAWEED

The coastline and open water of the Hebrides is rich with marine algae, the collective name for seaweed. Many types are found here including green, red and brown, with over 389 species recorded. Seaweed is used as food for both humans and livestock; as a fertiliser in the old run-rig system and for modern farming today; it was burnt to provide alkali for making soap and glass, and iodine was extracted from it. Today it makes a significant economic impact in the Hebrides. It's exported as fertiliser and dried as a nutritious snack, it's used in processed foods; as a biofuel; as a cosmetic and in skincare products. With the increase in the popularity of foraging you will often see people in the littoral zone in rocky areas as the tide goes out wearing wellingtons with scissors and a plastic bucket in hand gathering it to make into a variety of highly nutritious and tasty umami meals. Seaweed also makes beautiful macro studies.

It's quite apt that the authors of the best books about identifying, the history of, foraging for, and cooking with seaweed live in the Hebrides – both books are highly recommended.

Miek Zwamborm, who lives on Mull, is the author of *The Seaweed Collector's Handbook*, and Fiona Bird, who lives on Uist, is the author of *Seaweed in the Kitchen*.

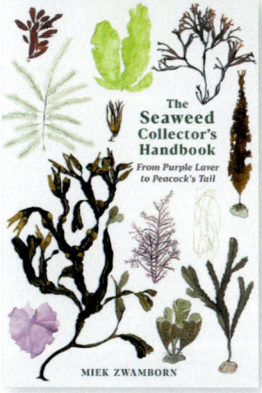

CLASSIC OUTER HEBRIDES LOCATIONS

There are so many classic locations to visit and photograph in the Outer Hebrides, it is difficult to whittle it down to a top ten. Here is a mix of my personal favourites and those that are well-known and considered classic. If your visit is short, make sure to put these on your itinerary. These are not in order of rank.

#	Location	Island	Page
1	Bhaltos Peninsula	Lewis	92
2	Boreray and the stacks	St Kilda	302
3	Bosta Beach	Great Bernera	88
4	Callanish	Lewis	78
5	Luskentyre	Harris	116
6	Prince Charlie's Beach	Eriskay	248
7	Ruabhal	Benbecula	222
8	Tràigh Hornais	North Uist	200
9	Tràigh Iar	Berneray	188
10	West Coast	Barra	264

1 BHALTOS PENINSULA — P.92

2 BORERAY AND THE STACKS — P.302

3 BOSTA BEACH — P.88

4 CALLANISH — P.78

CLASSIC OUTER HEBRIDES LOCATIONS 47

OUTER HEBRIDES NORTH: LEWIS AND HARRIS

Rushing waves at Bagh Steinigidh. Fujifilm X–T2, 10–24mm f/4, ISO 200, 3.7s at f/5.6. Jun.

Stac a'Phris on the west coast of Lewis. Fujifilm X–T2, 14mm f/2.8, ISO 200, 1s at f/11. Sep.

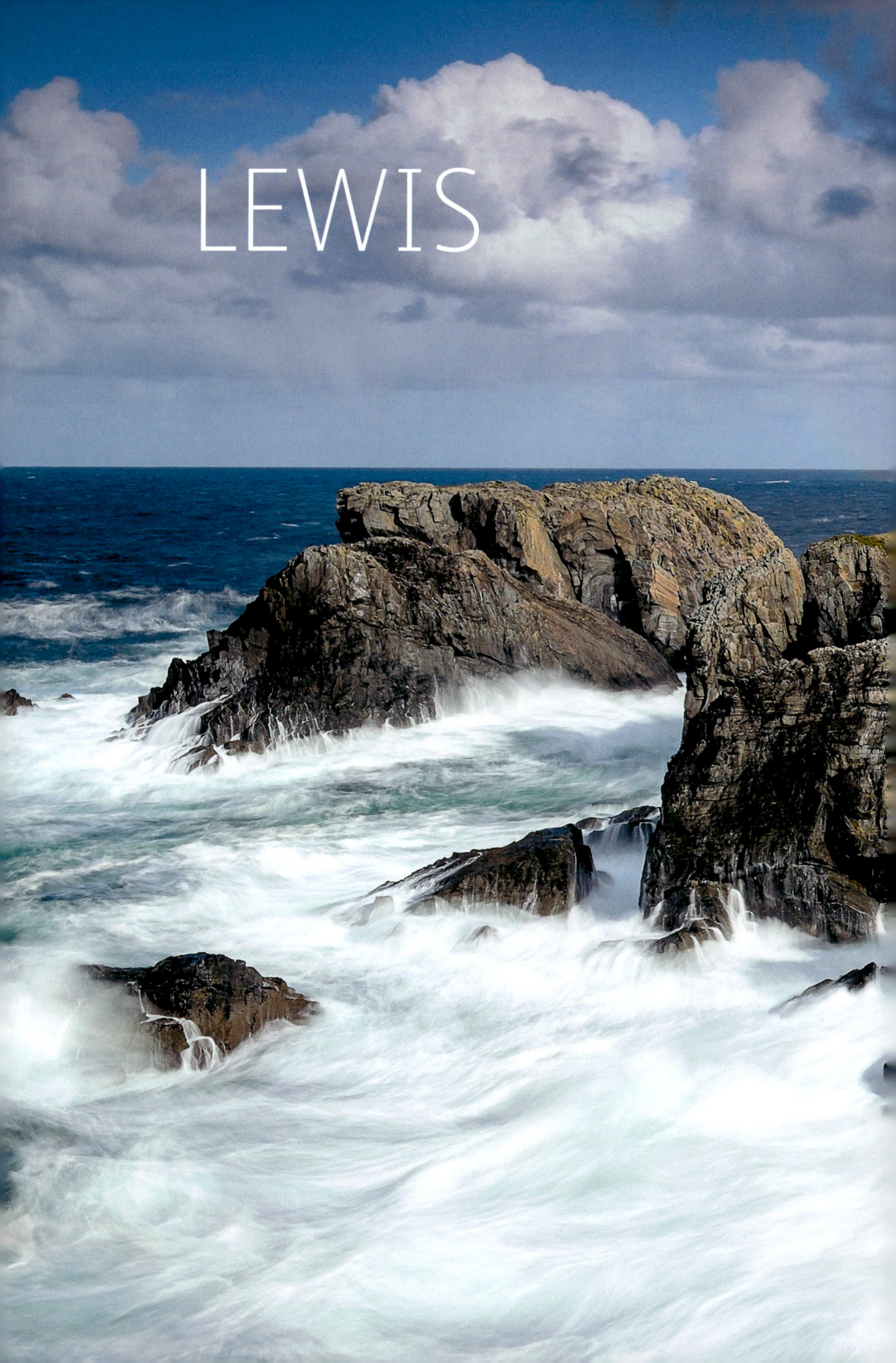

LEWIS – INTRODUCTION

The Isle of Lewis is the most northerly and largest island in the Outer Hebrides. It is a fascinating island, a heady mix of ancient culture and scenic coastlines, uninhabited peatlands and barren hills. An island which can appear austere in some lights and joyful in others, with weather that can change in an instant as it barrels in off the Atlantic. It is a stronghold of the Gaelic culture, preserving its traditions and way of life; crofting, weaving and fishing are still features of the local industry.

Lewis still feels relatively quiet in terms of visitors and apart from the obvious destination of Callanish, you are often likely to have some of the finest locations all to yourself, especially out of summer. The island is served by the Caledonian MacBrayne ferry from Ullapool on the mainland to the islands main town of Stornaway. This runs twice a day and takes 2hrs 45m. Stornaway is a bustling town with a busy harbour and should provide everything you will need for your stay on the island. Outside of Stornaway there are a number of smaller local shops within local communities.

Photographically the island offers huge variety. The west coast has a number of fine beaches and rugged coastal drama like the impressive Stac a'Phris arch which reaches out into the Atlantic. There is the Butt of Lewis lighthouse with its dramatic cliffs, notoriously the windiest place in the UK. On the east coast there is the huge sandy beach of Tràigh Mhor at Tolsta which offers a fantastic panoramic view of the mainland hills across the Minch. Or just to the north, the smaller Garry Beach, studded with sea stacks and caves, a veritable playground to explore. Way out west there is the huge expanse of Uig sands, where the Lewis Chessmen, lost by the Vikings, were discovered. There is the Bhaltos peninsula, with one of the finest Hebridean beaches of them all at Riof. To the south of Uig there are the Mangurstadh stacks, dramatic rock pinnacles standing in a furious sea where on a particularly clear day you may catch a glimpse of St Kilda far off on the Atlantic horizon.

Then there are the historical and cultural sites of Lewis. The Neolithic standing stones at Callanish; enigmatic, ancient, unknowable and beautiful. A site to be savoured at dawn and dusk with the hope of fleeting light catching the top of the stones. Or the broch at Dun Carloway with its fine view south across the land and out to sea. There is the blackhouse village at Gearrnan, with its restored thatched roof buildings providing a glimpse into the past. There is the Time and Tide Bell on the beach at Bosta on Great Bernera which tolls a warning to us about the dangers of climate change and rising sea levels.

The bedrock of the island is Lewissian Gneiss, the barebones of the earth. Up to 3000 million years old, formed through folding, compression and heating. Patterned and striped, sometimes with intense colours, these rocks appear throughout the Outer Hebrides and they provide hard to resist as subjects themselves or as foreground elements. There are some incredible examples at Ardroil beach in Uig.

How to get to Lewis

Ferry

There are frequent Calmac sailings from Ullapool on the mainland to Stornoway, Lewis (2hrs 45m); or Uig on Skye to Tarbert on Harris (2hrs 15m). From landing on Harris, it is possible to drive north onto Lewis. Ullapool is 233 miles from Glasgow (4+ hrs) and 211 Miles from Edinburgh (4+ hrs), and public transport to Ullapool is provided by Citylink (bus). There are no rail links to Ullapool, the nearest station is at Garve which is 25 miles from Inverness on the A835 and 31 miles from Ullapool. You can catch a Citylink bus to Ullapool from Garve.

Air

Lewis airport is located just outside Stornaway and is served by Loganair.co.uk, Flybe, Eastern Airways and Highlands and Islands Airports Limited (HIA).

Previous spread: The Butt of Lewis lighthouse. Fujifilm X–T2, 18–55mm f/2.8–f/4, ISO 200, 1.8s at f/8. Sep.

LEWIS	
Scottish Gaelic	Leòdhas.
Area	683 sq. miles (1768 sq. km).
Length/breadth	36 × 14 miles.
Highest Elevation	Mealaisbhal, 574m (1,883ft).
Owned by	Community/private residents. Comhairle nan Eilean Siar, the Western Isles Council.
Population	19,658
Largest settlement(s)	Stornoway (Steòrnabhagh), villages: North Tolsta, Carloway and Leurbost with significant populations.
Vehicles allowed	Yes
Car/Bike rental	Bernera Bikes (Kirkibost), Bespoke Bicycle, Bike Hebrides (Stornoway). Car hire *carhire-hebrides.co.uk*
Public transport	Yes. Bus timetable at *cne-siar.gov.uk*
Day trips from mainland?	No
Internet/mobile phone coverage	Broadband. 3G/4G dependent on carrier. Poor or no reception away from main towns. Public wifi at ferry terminals and some businesses.
Power	Grid and planned renewable sources (wind).
Island website(s)	*isle-of-lewis.com* • *visitouterhebrides.co.uk* • *visitscotland.com* *scotland.org.uk* • *undiscoveredscotland.co.uk*
Festivals/Events	Midnight Sun Festival, Stornoway (May) • HebCelt Festival, Stornoway (July) *lanntair.com* • Outer Hebrides Wildlife Festival, all islands (July) • Faclan Book Festival (Oct/Nov) • Hebridean Dark Skies Festival (Feb) • Open Studios Hebrides (July) • Guided walks at RSPB Loch na Muilne Reserve • Hebridean Pride Festival (June). More at *visitouterhebrides.co.uk/whats-on* and *hebevents.com*
Accommodation	Book well in advance for: camping, B&Bs and hostels, self catering, boutique hotels and spa-spec chalets. *isle-of-lewis.com/accommodation* and *visitouterhebrides.co.uk*
Provisions/Eating Out	There are over 50 restaurants, pubs and cafes on Lewis. For a listing visit: *visitouterhebrides.co.uk*. There are several supermarkets in Stornaway.
Wildlife	Otters, red deer, seals, dolphins, harbour porpoise and several species of whales. Redshank, greenshank, oystercatcher, curlew, ringed plover and dunlin. Shelduck and red-breasted Merganser (fish-eating duck) are to be seen on Loch Erisort, and large numbers of greylag geese and lapwing are found throughout the district.
Night Sky Bortle Scale	Class 1 outside of Stornoways.

LOCATIONS

1. Tolsta and Garry 56
2. The Northernmost Point 62
3. Dail Mòr Dail Beag and Stac a' Phris 68
4. Village and Broch 74
5. Callanish 78
6. Great Bernera 86
7. The Bhaltos Peninsula 92
8. Uig 96
9. Mangersta 102

Maps

- OS Landranger Map 8 (1:50 000) Stornoway & North Lewis
- OS Landranger Map 13 (1:50 000) West Lewis & North Harris

1. TOLSTA AND GARRY

As you drive north from Stornoway you will eventually reach the crofting village of Tolsta, strung out along the top of the cliffs facing the mainland. As the houses become more sparse the road narrows and sweeps downhill to the incredible beach Tràigh Mhor with over 2km of golden sand backed by dunes and crofts. Just around the corner is Tràigh Ghearadha or Garry Beach, an all together different beach, sheltered and secluded with hidden caves and towering spires of rock. Together they make a lovely couple of sandy beaches with an outlook to the east which is very unusual for the Outer Hebrides.

What to shoot and viewpoints

Viewpoint 1 – Tràigh Mhor

From the car park a path winds its way onto the beach alongside a peat-brown stream which burbles and braids across the sand at the northern end of the shore. The beach itself requires some height to experience the full sweep of sand, and a quick scramble up the dunes provides a lovely vantage point. Across the Minch, the Sutherland hills appear etched across the skyline with the shapely Suilven showing why it is named the Sugar Loaf. At dawn especially this can be a striking silhouette. »

Looking south along Tràigh Mhor from the dunes (VP1). Fujifilm X–T2, 18–55mm f/2.8–f/4, ISO 200, 1/1700s at f/8. Sep.

How to get here

From Stornoway head north on the A857 to Barabhas and Ness before turning right onto the B895 at Newmarket which is signposted Tolstadh. Follow the road for 12 miles until the car park at Tràigh Mhor is reached. Tràigh Ghearadha is just around the headland. There are parking areas at both beaches.

Viewpoint 1 – Tràigh Mhor & Viewpoint 2 – Above Tràigh Mhor

- **Lat/Long**: 58.361340, -6.2165911
- **what3words**: ///factories.outwit.handicaps
- **Grid Ref**: NB534491
- **Postcode**: HS2 0NN

Viewpoint 3 – Tràigh Ghearadha Stacks & Viewpoint 4 – Above Tràigh Ghearadha

- **Lat/Long**: 58.367795, -6.2219615
- **what3words**: ///lace.insolvent.parked
- **Grid Ref**: NB532499
- **Postcode**: HS2 0NN

Accessibility

All the viewpoints are easily accessible with good paths from the parking areas. Some of the stacks at Tràigh Ghearadha can be inaccessible at high tide.

Best time of year/day

Facing roughly east, both of these beaches are fantastic before dawn as the rising sun perfectly silhouettes the mountains on the mainland. There are photographs to be had at any time of the year; either under bright blue skies of summer or the storm clouds of winter.

1 TOLSTA AND GARRY

Sheep with the Minch beyond. Fujifilm X–T2, 55–200mm f/3.5–f/4.8, ISO 200, 1/1800s at f/4.8. Sep.

Viewpoint 2 – Above Tràigh Mhor ♿

If the dunes haven't provided enough elevation for you then an alternative is to head back up to the road from the car park and follow it north. From this height the full length of the beach is revealed and on days of heavy swell it is a great spot to watch the breakers rolling in. »

Top left: *Tolsta Community Shop. Fujifilm X–T2, 18–55mm f/2.8–f/4, ISO 200, 1/350s at f/8. Sep.*

The grand sweep of Tràigh Mhor from the road (VP2). Fujifilm X–T2, 18–55mm f/2.8–f/4, ISO 200, 1/1800s at f/8. Sep.

1 TOLSTA AND GARRY

Light illuminates a passage through the rocks at Tràigh Ghearadha. Fujifilm X–T2, 18–55mm f/2.8–f/4, ISO 200, 1/10s at f/8. Sep.

Viewpoint 3 – Tràigh Ghearadha Stacks

Just around the headland is Tràigh Ghearadha, a smaller but no less dramatic beach. From the parking area head down to the gate and follow the path on to the foreshore, to the south your eye will be immediately drawn to the famous rock stacks which loom over the beach. The smallest of these is the obvious composition here, sitting furthest out from the cliffs and offering a nice focal point. At low tide it is possible to walk around the larger rock stacks and explore the cave which cuts through the largest of these.

Morning sun hits one of the stacks at Tràigh Ghearadha. Fujifilm X–T2, 18–55mm f/2.8–f/4, ISO 200, 1/120s at f/8. Sep.

A view of the stacks from the cliff above the beach. Fujifilm X–T2, 14mm f/2.8, ISO 200, 1/4s at f/8. Sep.

Viewpoint 4 – Above Tràigh Ghearadha

Another way to photograph the stacks is from the cliffs above. Retrace your steps back to the dunes and head up, following the edge of the cliff. From here it is possible to isolate the stacks against the beach, and turn them into a compelling foreground for the view north across the shore.

The solitary stack in the centre of Tràigh Ghearadha. Fujifilm X–T2, 18–55mm f/2.8–f/4, ISO 200, 0.5s at f/8. Sep.

2 THE NORTHERNMOST POINT

The north of Lewis isn't a beautiful Hebridean paradise. There aren't any chocolate-box villages or picture postcard beaches. However, it is an exhilarating place to visit. A hard landscape, the wind-blasted tip of the northernmost point of an island in the North Atlantic. The sea here is relentless, pounding the cliffs and beaches in an elemental battle of will. The north of Lewis resists, head down, getting on with the task of thriving in this unrelenting environment. One of the last areas of predominately Gaidhlig speakers, this part of Lewis has a distinct identity and takes pride in its unique traditions.

What to shoot and viewpoints

Viewpoint 1 – Port of Ness ♿

The community of Ness at the north of Lewis encompasses a number of crofting villages which line the A857 as it runs northeast. The sheltered harbour, Port of Ness is at the end of the road and offers the potential for studies of the boats and assorted marine gubbins like creels, ropes and buoys. To the south of the harbour is a lovely sandy beach which often attracts some powerful waves. »

Opposite top left: breakwater at the eastern end of the harbour at Port of Ness. Fujifilm X–T2, 18–55mm f/2.8–f/4, ISO 200, 1/60s at f/5.6. Sep. **Top right**: south along the beach, Fujifilm X–T2, 18–55mm f/2.8–f/4, ISO 200, 1/680s at f/8. Sep. **Middle left**: a shark? Fujifilm X–T2, 18–55mm f/2.8–f/4, ISO 200, 1/220s at f/10. Sep. **Middle right**: the harbour at Port of Ness. Fujifilm X–T2, 18–55mm f/2.8–f/4, ISO 200, 1/640s at f/10. Sep. **Bottom left**: angles on the breakwater. Fujifilm X–T2, 18–55mm f/2.8–f/4, ISO 200, 1/000s at f/10. Sep. **Bottom right**: waves breaking on the pier. Fujifilm X–T2, 18–55mm f/2.8–f/4, ISO 200, 1/630s at f/10. Sep.

How to get here

Despite being only 26 miles from Stornoway it feels like a long old drive to get to Port of Ness. The long straight roads of the west coast pass through a number of crofting settlements, surrounded by open moorland. On a sunny day it feels glorious; a lovely drive under a big sky but in the rain it can feel quite desolate. To reach Port of Ness head north from Stornoway on the A857 for 20 minutes. At Barvas bear right and continue on the A857 until Port of Ness where the road ends at the harbour. To reach The Butt of Lewis and Port Stoth head back along the A857 and take the first minor road on the right. This leads to Eoropie, where at the cross roads you can either turn right for the Butt of Lewis and Port Stoth (signposted Rubha Robhanais) or head straight on and follow the road round to the parking area at Eoropie beach.

Viewpoint 1 – Port of Ness

- **Lat/Long:** 58.493189, -6.2254545
- **what3words:** ///tastings.cheaper.logged
- **Grid Ref:** NB538638
- **Postcode:** HS2 0XA

Viewpoint 2 – Port Stoth

- **Lat/Long:** 58.510725, -6.2546302
- **what3words:** ///dustbin.voting.spurring
- **Grid Ref:** NB522659
- **Postcode:** HS2 0XH

Above: a sheltered garden in Port of Ness. Fujifilm X–T2, 18–55mm f/2.8–f/4, ISO 200, 1/230s at f/10. Sep.

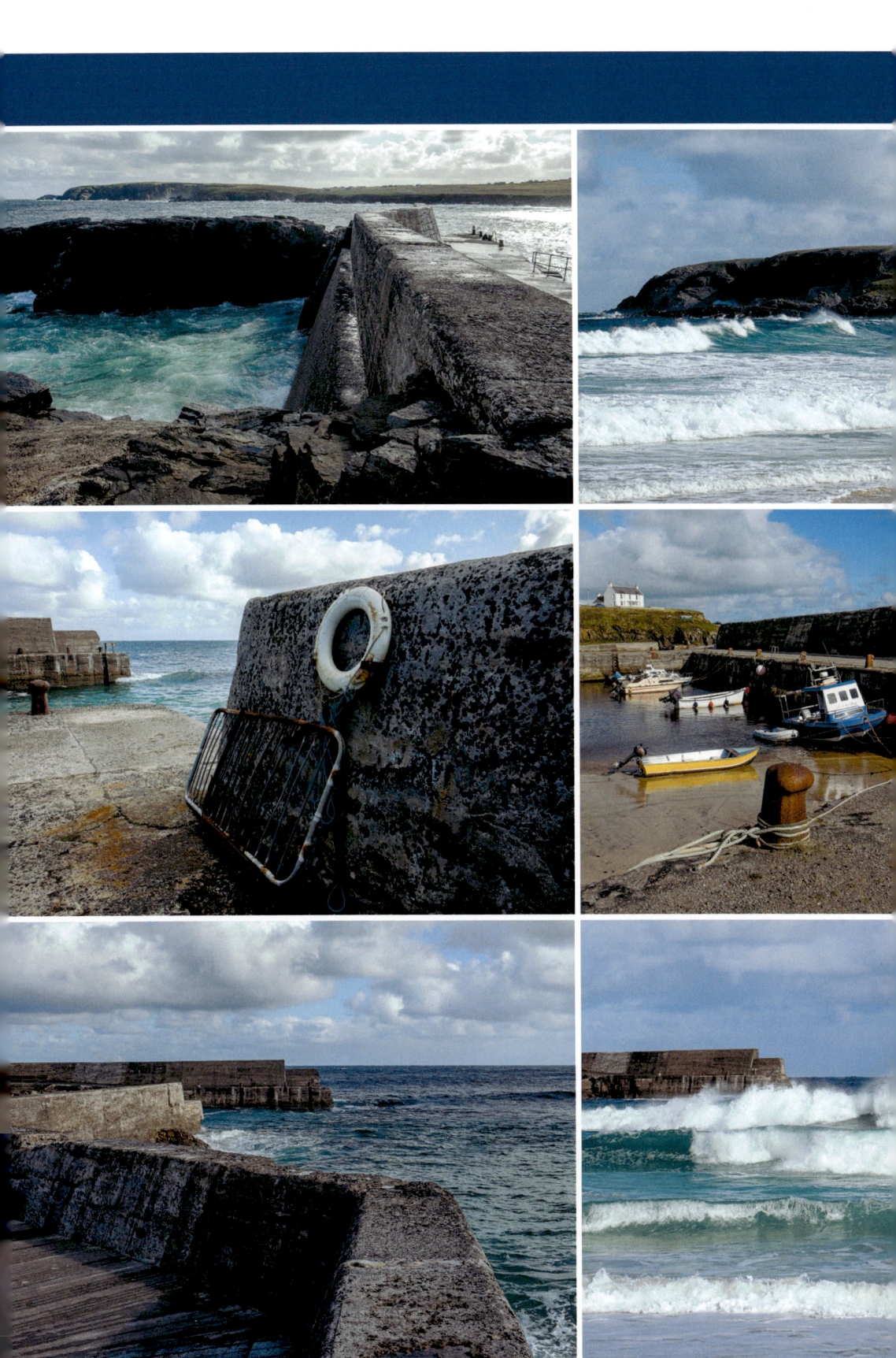

2 THE NORTHERNMOST POINT

The wee beach at Port Stoth. Fujifilm X–T2, 18–55mm f/2.8–f/4, ISO 200, 1/850s at f/8. Sep.

Wild sea to the west of The Butt of Lewis Lighthouse. Fujifilm X–T2, 18–55mm f/2.8–f/4, ISO 200, 4.5s at f/5.6. Sep.

Viewpoint 2 – Port Stoth

On the way to the Butt of Lewis the small beach and slipway at Port Stoth is passed. This was used to deliver by sea the materials for the building of the lighthouse as the road infrastructure wasn't suitable. The small brick storage building on the headland is a remnant of its previous use and provides a nice element in the view. A small sheltered cove, it supplies a nice alternative to the wilder beaches in its vicinity.

Viewpoint 3 – Butt of Lewis

As you arrive at the lighthouse your first task before getting out the car is to make sure your hat fits. If it's not tight enough then the wind will snatch it off your head and it will be at Cape Wrath before you know it. Yes it's often windy at the Butt of Lewis. In fact it was named the Windiest Place in the UK by The Guinness Book of Records. The first spot you will be drawn to is the cliff edge opposite the car park. The cliffs here present a tortured and

Viewpoint 3 – Butt of Lewis

- **Lat/Long:** 58.514899, -6.2602705
- **what3words:** ///mallets.chapels.talkative
- **Grid Ref:** NB520664
- **Postcode:** HS2 0XH

Viewpoint 4 – Eoropie Beach

- **Lat/Long:** 58.500076, -6.2625303
- **what3words:** ///visitors.taskbar.hooked
- **Grid Ref:** NB517647
- **Postcode:** HS2 0XH

Accessibility

All the viewpoints are easily accessed from their parking areas and images can be made very close to the car if you should choose too. The cliffs at the Butt of Lewis can be very dangerous with slippery grass at the edges of drops and unpredictable gusts of wind. A lot of care should be taken here as fatal accidents could easily happen. The other viewpoints should pose no problems.

Best time of year/day

The Butt of Lewis is an excellent sunset and sunrise location, although will generally work at any time as the drama of the cliffs can make up for lack of golden light. Stormy conditions with huge waves makes for dramatic images but would definitely increase the level of danger. On such days a visit to Eoropie or Port of Ness would be less risky. There is good potential at dawn at Port of Ness to catch the sun rising over the hills of Sutherland across The Minch.

2 THE NORTHERNMOST POINT

Windbreak seat at Eoropie Beach. Fujifilm X–T2, 18–55mm f/2.8–f/4, ISO 200, 1/150s at f/10. Sep.

convoluted appearance with the strata stripped bare. It works on a number of levels from macro studies of the layers of rock to wider vistas of the coastline. Heading around the northern side of the lighthouse reveals rock stacks, vertiginous drops and on most days, rough seas dashing themselves against the cliffs. Exploring along the grassy edge of the cliffs will reveal many excellent spots to photograph the lighthouse, siting in splendid isolation above the maelstrom.

Viewpoint 4 – Eoropie Beach

If you are craving some softness after the harsh landscape of the Butt, then Eoropie can perhaps provide it; depending on the direction of the wind! Some lovely dunes and a wide sandy bay provide plenty of opportunities and the jumbled roofs of the croft houses to the south make an interesting horizon.

Top: the lighthouse from the cliffs to the east. Fujifilm X–T2, 18–55mm f/2.8–f/4, ISO 200, 1/230s at f/10. Sep. Middle: the rugged coastline to the west of the lighthouse. Fujifilm X–T2, 18–55mm f/2.8–f/4, ISO 200, 1/450 at f/11. Sep. Bottom: football pitch near Ness FC. Fujifilm X–T2, 18–55mm f/2.8–f/4, ISO 200, 1/120s at f/11. Sep.

Opposite: crofthouses on the skyline seen from Eoropie Beach. Fujifilm X–T2, 55–200mm f/3.5–f/4.8, ISO 200, 1/1800s at f/5.6. Sep.

3. DAIL MÒR, DAIL BEAG AND STAC A' PHRIS

Dail Mòr and Dail Beag are two fantastic beaches on the west coast of Lewis which provide many opportunities for great seascape photography. As the names suggest, one is big (Mòr) and one is small (Beag) and both have their own individual charms. These two sandy beaches punctuate some incredibly rugged cliffs and can be linked by an excellent coastal walk which runs from Gearrannan to Bragar. To the north west is Stac a Phris, a phenomenal piece of natural rock architecture jutting out into the Atlantic and one which is not to be missed by those who appreciate a bit of drama.

What to shoot and viewpoints

Viewpoint 1 – Dail Mòr

If you've arrived at Dalmore on a calm day you have missed some of its delights. On stormy days the waves crashing against the cliffs and thudding into the sand give it a fantastically rugged and wild feel. There are a number of good opportunities on the beach itself as the burn snakes down across the sand, or along the top of the beach where wave-smoothed boulders provide a great foreground for some long exposure work. The cliffs at either end of the beach can be accessed; to the west a steep track ascends to the cliff top, providing a great view of the entire beach. Alternatively a more sedate path from the car park leads up to the western cliffs; follow the yellow topped posts. The north eastern cliffs are incredibly dramatic with intricately folded metamorphic rocks in hues of red and orange which tower above a turbulent sea. Follow the beachside path beside the cemetery and up the steep track to reach the clifftop. Be careful on the slippery path and if unsure of your footing stay well back from the edge. It is possible to follow the path right round to Dail Beag. »

Dail Mòr beach. Fujifilm X–T2, 18–55mm f/2.8–f/4, ISO 200, 1/250s at f/8. Sep.

How to get here

Head north from Stornoway Harbour and take the A859 south, signposted for Tarbert. After 15 minutes after passing a garage and a row of houses take the A858 west, passing Callanish and Carloway. After 25 minutes Dail More is signposted to the right. To reach Dail Beag, follow the A858 past this junction and take the next minor road on the left.

Viewpoint 1 – Dail Mòr

- **Lat/Long**: 58.305081, -6.7526905
- **what3words**: ///interrupt.reminder.revealing
- **Grid Ref**: NB217450
- **Postcode**: HS2 9AE

Viewpoint 2 – Dail Beag & Viewpoint 3 – Stac a' Phris

- **Lat/Long**: 58.312936, -6.7349445
- **what3words**: ///request.broadens.unhappy
- **Grid Ref**: NB228458
- **Postcode**: HS2 9AE

Accessibility

Both of the beaches can be accessed on good paths from their respective car parks, however, the cliffs on either side are steep with some slippery grass paths. The route to Stac a' Phris is relatively pathless and boggy but the yellow topped posts aid route finding. The jumbled clifftop boulders where the best views of the stack are can be slippery and precarious; be very careful in this location, especially before dawn or after sunset.

Best time of year/day

The beaches themselves are best at sunset, at dawn the low hills to the east block the early light, however, Stac a' Phris works best at sunrise, as at sunset you may find yourself shooting into the sun. It can work under overcast conditions though. All the viewpoints work well with a stormy sea which can heighten the drama of the rugged coastal landscape.

Above: *the boulders at the top of Dail Mòr beach. Fujifilm X–T2, 18–55mm f/2.8–f/4, ISO 200, 1.2s at f/11. Sep.* ***Below***: *stormy sea at Dail Mòr. Fujifilm X–T2, 18–55mm f/2.8–f/4, ISO 200, 1s at f/10. Sep.*

3 DAIL MÒR, DAIL BEAG AND STAC A' PHRIS

Top: *abandoned croft house near Dail Beag. Fujifilm X–T2, 18–55mm f/2.8–f/4, ISO 200, 1/3s at f/10. Sep.*

Above left: *rock stack at the southern end of Dail Beag beach. Fujifilm X–T2, 18–55mm f/2.8–f/4, ISO 200, 1/640s at f/7.1. Sep.*

Viewpoint 2 – Dail Beag

Unless you have walked around the coast from Dail Mòr the approach to Dail Beag takes you down a single track road past a pretty loch. The loch itself offers some interest with its reed fringed edges providing a lovely foil to the rugged hills behind. From the small car park at the end of the road a path crosses the burn and takes you down onto the small sandy bay. Like Dail Mor it features some wonderful smooth boulders along the high tide line. The beach itself is small and enclosed by the cliffs either side,

Above: peaty water flowing across the sand at Dail Beag. Fujifilm X–T2, 18–55mm f/2.8–f/4, ISO 200, 1/400s at f/8. Sep.

and has the feel of a natural amphitheater stepping down to the sea. The rock stacks on the south western side make a good subject when the sea is crashing against them especially when shot from the north western side of the beach. It is possible to follow the path on the south western side with leads up past some ruined croft houses onto the top of the cliffs and get a view looking down onto the stack. »

3 DAIL MÒR, DAIL BEAG AND STAC A' PHRIS

Top: the moorland above Dail Beag. Fujifilm X–T2, 14mm f/2.8, ISO 200, 1/3s at f/10. Sep.

Above left: the rocky cliff edge at Stac a'Phris (VP3). Fujifilm X–T2, 14mm f/2.8, ISO 200, 1s at f/10. Sep.

Viewpoint 3 – Stac a' Phris

The crowning glory of this rugged stretch of coastline is Stac a Phris; a natural arch thrusting out into the sea. It is best reached from Dail Beag where the coastal path can be picked up along the top of the shore. The yellow-topped timber posts lead you up the steep cliffs and across the moorland above. The Stack comes into view after roughly 2km, however, if you deviate from the posts to follow the

Above: Stac a'Phris (VP3). Fujifilm X–T2, 14mm f/2.8, ISO 200, 1.5s at f/10. Sep.

edge of the cliffs you will eventually reach it. An area of large sharp boulders steps down towards the cliff edge and provides plenty of scope to create a foreground to the stack. It's a dramatic location and with the right combination of light, tide and waves can be really special. On a clear day the Flannan Isles should be visible on the horizon some 50km off shore to the west.

4 VILLAGE AND BROCH

If you've had your fill of rugged cliffs and wave lashed sandy beaches these two spots should be right up your street. Two nice sedate viewpoints to recharge the batteries and learn about the ancient human history of this island.

What to shoot and viewpoints

Viewpoint 1 – Gearrannan Blackhouse Village ♿

As you travel around the Hebrides you will know doubt have noticed the ruins of the old Black Houses. Sometimes they have been restored, but usually their tumbledown walls are found on crofts next to the new and improved white houses. A long, low structure comprising dry stone walls and a thatched roof weighed down by boulders, the blackhouse provided snug accommodation for generations of Hebridean people and their livestock. Amazingly some of the blackhouses at Gearrannan were occupied up until the 1970s. They have now been sympathetically restored, providing holiday accommodation, a museum and a shop. The buildings are clustered around a winding road which eventually leads down to a stony shore and the thatched roofs, stonework, stacks of peat and deep set windows make for interesting studies, whatever the weather. It is also possible to get a wider view of the village and the coast from above by taking the path which climbs onto the shoulder beside the car park. »

Top: stacked peat at Gearrannan Blackhouse Village (VP1). Fujifilm X–T2, 18–55mm f/2.8–f/4, ISO 200, 1/500s at f/8. Sep.
Above: new thatch on the blackhouse. Fujifilm X–T2, 18–55mm f/2.8–f/4, ISO 200, 1/340s at f/5.6. Sep.

How to get here

Head north from Stornoway Harbour and take the A859 south, signposted for Tarbert. Fifteen minutes after passing a garage and a row of houses take the A858 west, passing Callanish. Before reaching Carloway a minor road on the left leads you to the signposted Dùn Chàrlabhaigh / Dun Carloway where there is car park and toilet block. For Gearrannan Blackhouse Village continue through Carloway, take the minor road on the left as on approaching Carloway FC football pitch. Follow this road until the Carloway Mill and take a left at the junction. Gearrannan Blackhouse Village and a small car park is at the end of the road.

Viewpoint 1 – Gearrannan Blackhouse Village

- **Lat/Long**: 58.296416, -6.7909107
- **what3words**: ///improving.embellish.pinches
- **Grid Ref**: NB193441
- **Postcode**: HS2 9AL

Viewpoint 2 – Dun Carloway

- **Lat/Long**: 58.268607, -6.7910926
- **what3words**: ///hazy.required.truckload
- **Grid Ref**: NB191411
- **Postcode**: HS2 9AZ

Accessibility

Each viewpoint is easily accessed from their respective parking areas with good paths underfoot.

Best time of year/day

Both of these locations are on the west coast so make good spots for sunset, however, they can work in all conditions really and may be saved for an overcast day. However, the dawn light illuminating the western face of Dùn Chàrlabhaigh is particularly appealing and may be worth exploring once the scaffolding is removed and the works are complete.

Looking across the roofs of Gearrannan Blackhouse Village. Fujifilm X-T2, 18–55mm f/2.8–f/4, ISO 200, 1/320s at f/8. Sep.

4 VILLAGE AND BROCH

Stone outcrop at the base of the broch. Fujifilm X–T2, 18–55mm f/2.8–f/4, ISO 200, 1/100s at f/8. Sep.

Viewpoint 2 – Dun Carloway

Dùn Chàrlabhaigh or Dun Carloway is a broch built in first century AD which sits on a small rise overlooking Loch an Dùin. Currently it is undergoing restoration to stabilise the structure, however, it is still located at a wonderful lookout point with far reaching views across the intricate coastline of Lewis and Great Bernera. A broch is a fortified tower, usually formed of two concentric circular drystone walls and they can be found throughout Scotland in various states of disrepair. They are fascinating structures and the fact there are many are still standing is a testament to the craft of the Iron Age builders. This broch was once used as a stronghold by the cattle rustling Morrison's of Ness who, after stealing from the MacAuleys of Uig holed up in the structure thinking the 14m high walls would offer protection from the irate clan. However, Donald Cam MacCauley had other ideas. He climbed the broch using two daggers and smoked the thieving Morrison's out with burning bunches of heather! The MacAuleys then wrecked the broch, which does seem a bit unreasonable. The best location for a shot of the broch is found on the higher ground to the right of the access path. A smaller path branches off the main path and rises to a higher point giving a fantastic vantage point of the broch and the wider landscape. There is also scope for detail shots at the broch itself, particularly appealing are the areas where the natural rock outcrops have been incorporated into the stonework.

Top: *Dun Carloway from the hillside above (VP2). Fujifilm X–T2, 18–55mm f/2.8–f/4, ISO 200, 1/300s at f/8. Sep.* **Above**: *the edge of the broch. Fujifilm X–T2, 18–55mm f/2.8–f/4, ISO 200, 1/230s at f/8. Sep.*

Opposite: *a walk around the Gearrannan Blackhouse Village provides plenty of interest.*

5. CALLANISH

Nobody completely understands stone circles. We know roughly when they were constructed; where the rocks came from and sometimes how they align with astral bodies. But nobody knows the true reason behind them and why certain locations like Callanish were so sacred to the people who lived here nearly 5000 years ago. There are over twenty megalithic sites located within a 2 mile radius of Callanish so perhaps there was something of particular importance in the landscape which drove the ancient people to build these monuments here. Of all the megalithic sites in the area, and perhaps even the UK, Callanish is the most complex and dramatic. It has a unique atmosphere and engenders a hushed reverence, particularly after sunset and before sunrise when the mysterious stones appear silhouetted against the sky.

What to shoot and viewpoints

Viewpoint 1 – Callanish I
Approaching from the visitor centre you arrive at the southern end of the circle and are greeted with a breathtaking sight. An almost bewildering arrangement of massive monoliths which jostle for attention, eliciting feelings of awe, wonder and a deep respect for the people who undertook the superhuman effort of erecting them. At the centre your eye is drawn to a single monolith standing almost 5m high which is orientated on the north–south axis. Around this, lines of smaller stones reach out into the landscape forming a cruciform shape and creating a feeling of procession to the largest central stone. The stones themselves are Lewisian Gneiss, one of the oldest rocks on the planet, in a range of irregular shapes with surfaces weathered into elaborate and beautiful patterns. It is worth spending some quality time here walking the avenues, soaking up the atmosphere and exploring the stones before immediately getting the camera out. The stones have been here for thousands of years and they aren't going anywhere so there is no need to rush! Photographing a scene as complex as this can be quite tricky, especially if you are trying to shoot with a wider angle. The key is to try and separate the stones, perhaps concentrating on smaller groupings or even on some of the details in the stones themselves. The low sun at dawn or dusk can create some dramatic shadows which draw the eye into the circle, however, if you aren't blessed with great light then long exposures can heighten the ethereal nature of the stones lending an air of time passing, which is apt for these ancient stones. »

How to get here
Head north from Stornoway Harbour and take the A859 south, signposted for Tarbert. After 15 minutes after passing a garage and a row of houses take the A858 west, as you approach Callanish, at a bend in the road turn left. You will see the stones up on the small hill. Follow the road through the village and the visitor centre car park is on your left. Callanish II can be walked to from Callanish I or there is a small car park. Head back to A858 and turn right, Callanish II is reached via the next minor road on the right.

Viewpoint 1 – Callanish I & Viewpoint 2 – The Wider Landscape

- **Lat/Long**: 58.195681, -6.7435670
- **what3words**: ///simulations.heats.tune
- **Grid Ref**: NB213328
- **Postcode**: HS2 9DY

Viewpoint 3 – Callanish II

- **Lat/Long**: 58.195570, -6.7289335
- **what3words**: ///florists.seabirds.exacts
- **Grid Ref**: NB222327
- **Postcode**: HS2 9DY

Accessibility
There is a great visitor centre at Callanish, with a car park, toilets and cafe. From here it is a short stroll up a well made path to the stones. There is a kissing gate which gives access to the stones, however this may be difficult for wheelchair users. Therefore the gated access from the small car park to the north of the stones may be more suitable than the route up from the visitor centre. The short walk to Callanish II is pathless and can be quite boggy.

Best time of year/day
As the stones sit on a rise amongst relatively flat land to the east and west they make the ideal location for sunrise and sunset, catching the light at both ends of the day. The location is popular at all times and you may find yourself sharing the scene with other photographers and perhaps even some druids at the solstice. However, with some careful composition you should be able to hide people behind the stones. The stones also lend themselves to be being photographed in the blue hours, with their distinctive shapes silhouetted against the sky. Should you visit in the winter, it would be a fantastic place to witness if the northern lights are putting on a show.

Above: looking along the central axis of Callanish I in the mist (VP1). Fujifilm X–T2, 55–200mm f/3.5–f/4.8, ISO 200, 1/100s at f/4.5. Sep

The stones make a fascinating composition as a group, but there are also numerous other compositions to be found amongst the stones.

5 CALLANISH

A ruined croft house to the south east of Callanish (VP2). Fujifilm X–T2, 55–200mm f/3.5–f/4.8, ISO 200, 1/8s at f/8. Sep.

Viewpoint 2 – The wider landscape

The stones sit on a promontory which juts out into the loch and a small knoll to the south of the entrance gate provides a fantastic lookout point. From here you can gaze across to the Clisham on Harris, to the mountains around Uig and south east to the myriad shimmering lochans amongst the moorland. A ruined croft house stands across the water, its empty windows blankly gazing out towards Callanish. There are numerous vignettes which can be picked out with a long lens in this landscape. »

Looking across to the Harris hills above the mist. Fujifilm X–T2, 55–200mm f/3.5–f/4.8, ISO 200, 1/45s at f/8. Sep.

Lochs, moorland and hills south east of Callanish. Fujifilm X–T2, 55–200mm f/3.5–f/4.8, ISO 200, 1/50s at f/8. Sep

5 CALLANISH

A cow uses an ancient neolithic standing stone as a scratching post at Callanish II (VP3). Fujifilm X–T2, 55–200mm f/3.5–f/4.8, ISO 200, 1/500s at f/4.5. Sep.

Viewpoint 3 – Callanish II

Visible from Callanish to the east is Callanish II, another intriguing ancient stone circle. The stones here range from two to three metres in height and are arranged in a rough ellipse. They are enclosed within a fence, but you will often find cows amongst them, scratching their flanks along the well-worn sides of the stones. Whilst not as dramatic or complex as Callanish I, it is definitely worth a visit. Just to the south is a ruined croft house, its steel roof gradually rusting to the colour of the autumn hills.

Hide and seek at Callanish II. Fujifilm X–T2, 55–200mm f/3.5–f/4.8, ISO 200, 1/850s at f/4.8. Sep.

Opposite: abandoned croft house near Callanish II. Fujifilm X–T2, 18–55mm f/2.8–f/4, ISO 200, 1/300s at f/5.6. Sep.

6 GREAT BERNERA

The island of Great Bernera offers a variety of opportunities to the photographer who wants to explore. With a number of interesting historical sites, and an incredible beach with a unique tidal sculpture at its northern tip there really is something for everyone. For a relatively small island it has a thriving population, school, shop and post office. A fantastic island and one not to be missed on the route out west.

What to shoot and viewpoints

Viewpoint 1 – The Bernera Bridge and Callanish VIII

The Bernera Bridge connects the island to Lewis and its construction in 1953 was vital to the long term prospects of the island. There are numerous islands around the Hebrides which previously supported relatively large populations but due to a lack of connectivity became less desirable and eventually became uninhabited. The residents of Bernera clearly feared this and even threatened to dynamite the cliffs and create their own causeway if a bridge wasn't constructed. From the Bernera side of the bridge a series of small steps leads up the cliff to a gate which opens out onto Callanish VIII, a semi-circle of four standing stones. This outpost of the Callanish system frames a lovely view westwards to the Uig hills. »

Looking towards the bridge from Callanish VIII. Fujifilm X–T2, 18–55mm f/2.8–f/4, ISO 200, 1/800s at f/5.6. Sep.

How to get here

Head north from Stornoway Harbour and take the A859 south, signposted for Tarbert. Fifteen minutes after passing a garage and a row of houses take the A858 west, until at Garrynahine turn left onto the B8011. After 5 minutes turn right onto the B8059 at Bernera Junction and the bridge is a further 10 minutes to the north. There is parking on the Bernera side of the bridge just to the right as you arrive on the island. Bosta is situated at the end of the main road north through the island which passes through the village of Breaclait.

Viewpoint 1 – The Bernera Bridge and Callanish VIII

- **Lat/Long:** 58.205673, -6.8283102
- **what3words:** ///gamer.merge.gloves
- **Grid Ref:** NB164342
- **Postcode:** HS2 9LP

Viewpoint 2 – Bosta Beach & Viewpoint 3 – Bosta headland

- **Lat/Long:** 58.256046, -6.8786080
- **what3words:** ///bugs.stuck.lighters
- **Grid Ref:** NB139400
- **Postcode:** HS2 9LZ

Accessibility

Bosta beach is easily accessed with a large car park situated just above the beach, the headland is a bit more tricky with steep paths and a rough, bouldery and boggy plateau. It can be tricky underfoot post sunset and pre-dawn so care is required at this viewpoint. Callanish VIII is reached by a couple of steep steps, but is essentially road-side.

Best time of year/day

Bosta Beach is roughly north facing and is quite enclosed by surrounding hills and the headland, as such it tends to be better when the sun is higher in the sky. The headland to the west catches the low morning and evening light and makes a perfect sunset location with a number of opportunities for compositions amongst the lochans and boulders. If you can time your visit to coincide with a high tide you will hear the sound of the Time and Tide Bell. It is worth visiting Callanish VIII at any time.

*Opposite top: the standing stones of Callanish VIII (VP1). Fujifilm X–T2, 18–55mm f/2.8–f/4, ISO 200, 1/500s at f/8. Sep.
Bottom: looking back to Lewis from Great Bernera. Fujifilm X–T2, 18–55mm f/2.8–f/4, ISO 200, 1/200s at f/5.6. Sep.*

6 GREAT BERNERA

Viewpoint 2 – Bosta Beach

The single track road which runs through the centre of Great Bernera gradually twists and turns over rocky ridges and alongside some lily strewn lochans, eventually terminating above the beach at Bosta. A path takes you alongside the cemetery drawing you down to a beautiful sheltered sandy bay. On a skerry just offshore is one of the Time and Tide Bells. There are number of these sculptures by the artist Marcus Vergette which have been sited around the UK coastline. At high tide the bells ring out, providing a reminder of the threat of rising sea level which faces coastal communities across the world. It catches the low evening sun and provides a lovely moment of intrigue in any picture in which it appears. The rocks along this stretch of the beach are particularly interesting and perfectly draw the eye to the sculpture. Tucked away at the southern end of the beach is a reconstruction of the Iron Age houses uncovered in 1993 by a storm which stripped the sand from the dunes. This discovery was studied by archaeologists and then buried again to preserve it and very little of it is now visible on the surface. The reconstructed house provides a nice anchor to the view north across the beach. »

Bosta beach and the Time and Tide Bell at dawn (VP2). Fujifilm X–T2, 18–55mm f/2.8–f/4, ISO 200, 240s at f/8. Sep.

Bosta beach from the dunes. Fujifilm X–T2, 18–55mm f/2.8–f/4, ISO 200, 1/240s at f/9. Sep.

Opposite left: the recreated Iron Age house and Bosta beach. Fujifilm X–T2, 18–55mm f/2.8–f/4, ISO 200, 1/340s at f/8. Sep.
Right: the Time and Tide Bell. Fujifilm X–T2, 18–55mm f/2.8–f/4, ISO 200, 1/180s at f/9. Sep.

6 GREAT BERNERA

Top: one of many reedy lochans on the headland at Bosta (VP3). Fujifilm X–T2, 18–55mm f/2.8–f/4, ISO 200, 1/15s at f/11. Sep.
Above: the reeds make for some great detail studies.

Opposite: looking out from the headland to the uninhabited isles off the coast. Fujifilm X–T2, 18–55mm f/2.8–f/4, ISO 200, 0.6s at f/11 Sep.

Viewpoint 3 – Bosta headland

The headland to the west of Bosta beach is accessed via a steep track which leads up from the Iron Age house. This gradually peters out amongst heather and boulder ground but it is easy enough to pick a route north across the flat plateau. There are some wonderful reedy lochans to explore and many erratics strewn around the surface which provide some foreground interest. Northwards, the view out to the uninhabited islands of Flodaigh, Bearasaigh and Seanna Chnoc is a delight. The headland also affords great views back down to Bosta beach.

7. THE BHALTOS PENINSULA

If you were to imagine a perfect Hebridean beach, you would probably be thinking of a beach like Reef. A perfect crescent of white shell sand, lapped by turquoise waters and backed by tousled marram grass dunes. Offshore, mysterious uninhabited islands shelter the beach from the swell, with the beach on Pabaigh Mòr appearing tantalisingly close. However, it's not the only draw on the Bhaltos peninsula, the popular surfing beach at Cliff offers a more rugged alternative and the monument of An Suileachan commemorating the historical events which have shaped the crofting community here provides a fantastic lookout over the peninsula.

What to shoot and viewpoints

Viewpoint 1 – Cliff Beach
The first beach you approach as you drive clockwise around the Bhaltos peninsula is Cliff. The parking area is located down a narrow track to the left of the circular peninsula road just before it starts to rise up. Enclosed by a high headland to the east and towering cliffs to the west it is a dramatic spot and attracts large and powerful waves. It is a favoured beach of surfers, and the viewpoint on the road which climbs up the eastern headland gives a great vantage point. The beach itself is quite difficult to photograph, there aren't many obvious focal points, however, the rocks and pools towards the western end provide some intrigue and with a long lens it is possible to capture action shots of the surfers. If you are very lucky you may sea the wreck of the Esra, a 19th century shipwreck which is occasionally exposed by the shifting sands and tides. »

How to get here
Special places often require longer journeys and the road to the Bhaltos peninsula is certainly a long one. Head north from Stornoway Harbour and take the A859 south, signposted for Tarbert. After 15 minutes after passing a garage and a row of houses take the A858 west, until at Garrynahine turn left onto the B8011. Follow this for 20 minutes until the narrow glen at Miavaig is reached and take a right onto the Bhaltos peninsula. A circular road takes you around the peninsula and it is recommended to follow a clockwise route, heading first to Cliff and then onto Bhaltos and Reef.

Viewpoint 1 – Cliff Beach
- Lat/Long: 58.220275, -6.9656516
- what3words: ///kindness.selection.hissing
- Grid Ref: NB085364
- Postcode: HS2 9HP

Viewpoint 2 – Reef Beach
- Lat/Long: 58.215794, -6.9363306
- what3words: ///flitting.broke.front
- Grid Ref: NB102358
- Postcode: HS2 9HS

Above: the sandy bay of Cliff beach (VP1). Fujifilm X–T2, 18–55mm f/2.8–f/4, ISO 200, 1/180s at f/8. Sep.

Far left: surfer at Cliff. Fujifilm X–T2, 55–200mm f/3.5–f/4.8, ISO 200, 1/1700s at f/4.8. Sep.

Left: the old oyster shed. Fujifilm X–T2, 18–55mm f/2.8–f/4, ISO 200, 1/250s at f/8. Sep.

7 THE BHALTOS PENINSULA

Looking across to Pabaigh Mòr from Reef beach. Fujifilm X–T2, 18–55mm f/2.8–f/4, ISO 200, 1/10s at f/9. Sep.

Top left: *Reef beach from the atop the headland to the east. Fujifilm X–T2, 18–55mm f/2.8–f/4, ISO 200, 1/1700s at f/5. Sep.*

Reef beach from the dunes towards the eastern end. Fujifilm X–T2, 18–55mm f/2.8–f/4, ISO 200, 1/640s at f/8. Sep.

Viewpoint 2 – Reef Beach

Marked on the OS map as Traigh na Beirigh, Reef beach can be accessed from the campsite, or the small parking area further along the road to the east. This second access point avoids the need to jump the small (but sometimes deep) stream which crosses the beach. The marram grass covered dunes offer up a great foreground to the sweep of white sand and catch the breeze beautifully on blustery days. It is also worth exploring the rockier areas at the western side of the beach, as these tumbled outcrops can provide a nice counterpoint to the soft white sand. At the eastern end of the shore a headland juts out in to the sea, providing a suitable end point to the beach and one which you will inevitably be drawn to walking towards. It is then possible to make your way up onto the promontory by following the track through the dunes and turning left up the steep slopes after the stile. The extra height gives a fantastic vantage point over the whole beach. Once up top, it is worth exploring around the headland, where a hidden sandy beach is located to the east.

Accessibility

Both beaches are served by adjacent parking areas, just a short hop across the dunes. The promontory at the eastern end of Reef beach can be steep and slippery although it is possible to stay back from the cliff edges. If exploring the western end of Cliff beach, be mindful of the tide as it is possible to get cut off.

Best time of year/day

These two beaches work at any time of the year, however, in summer the riot of colour provided by the machair and the seed heads of the marram grass swaying in the breeze can be really special. It is worth visiting Cliff on a day of big swell if you are planing on photographing the surfers. Reef beach catches the light at sunset or sunrise but equally looks stunning under a bright sun which heightens the dazzlingly white shell sand.

Opposite: *a tranquil evening in the dunes at Reef. Fujifilm X–T2, 18–55mm f/2.8–f/4, ISO 200, 230s at f/11. Sep.*

8 UIG

At the far western extremity of Lewis is a particularly special coastal landscape. A huge expanse of sand which is exposed twice daily by the tide, surrounded by dunes and backdropped to the south by bare elephant grey hills. It has a timeless quality to it, and under the summer sun the various turquoise hues of the shallow water in the bay is something to really savour. It covers a vast area and there are many opportunities both on the beach and on the headlands around it. The area is famed for the Lewis Chessmen; 12th century Norse chess pieces intricately carved from walrus tusk which were discovered buried in the sand. A life-size sculpture of one of the pieces can be seen on the way to the beach at Ardroil.

What to shoot and viewpoints

Viewpoint 1 – Ardroil

The simplest route onto the beach is at Ardroil where there is a campsite and a car park. The beach is accessed through a gate and via a path through the dunes. It is worth ascending the highest of the dunes to the south west to get an elevated view across the bay. On Druim Corcadale there are some large rock outcrops which jut out incongruously from the grass and can make an interesting focal point in the view. Uig Lodge appears in many views across the bay, its bright white walls standing out against the bare hillsides beyond. The dunes offer plenty of scope for compositions, particularly when the tide is fully in.

At the western end of the bay there are a number of rocky outcrops in the sand, which are in striking shades of pink and red. These work really well as foreground elements and pick up low light wonderfully. If the tide is out, walking across the bay is highly recommended. The rippled patterns of the sand often hold shapely pools of water and numerous detail studies can be had here. It is worth making for the small bridge across the far side of the bay, this gives access over a peaty stream to the far shore as well as providing further interest to images which look back across the beach. From here you can either retrace your steps back across the sand or head north across the elevated ground, eventually reaching the minor road. »

How to get here

Uig is quite a drive from Stornoway Harbour but is definitely worth it! (36 miles, takes just short of an hour). Head north from Stornoway and then take the A859 south, signposted for Tarbert. After 15 minutes after passing a garage and a row of houses take the A858 west, until at Garrynahine turn left onto the B8011. Follow this for 20 minutes and then on through the dramatic Gleann Bhaltois. On emerging from the glen the road begins to descend to the bay. Continue on past the shop and after 5 minutes you will reach a turning on the right which signposts you to the beach. There is parking at the end of this road at the campsite and the beach can be accessed through a gate on the opposite side of the road. Alternatively, walk back down the road to the statue of the Lewis Chessman where a gate gives access to the beach, and higher hillocks of Druim Corcadale. To get to Carnais, return to the main road and turn right. After the bridge turn right and follow the road on the western side of the bay. There is a small parking area to the side of the road. To get to the beach continue on foot past the house and barn on the right before taking the gate and path on the right.

Viewpoint 1 – Ardroil

Lat/Long:	58.184586, -7.0256389
what3words:	///again.rationing.physical
Grid Ref:	NB047327
Postcode:	HS2 9EU

Viewpoint 2 – Carnish Peninsula

Lat/Long:	58.176789, -7.0511806
what3words:	///tumblers.dock.inspector
Grid Ref:	NB031320
Postcode:	HS2 9EX

Accessibility

Both beaches are served by parking areas and are easily accessed via paths or across dunes. The route around the Carnish peninsula is pathless but it is relatively easy to follow the waters edge around to the starting point.

Best time of year/day

The beach at Uig offers opportunities at all times of the day; at sunrise and sunset the wider views are more attractive, however, there are images to be made here in any light conditions. The incredible rock textures and sand pattern can be enjoyed under dull flat light as much as under bright summer sun. Carnish is an obvious sunset destination, but there are still pictures to be had here at other times. There are also a huge variety of opportunities afforded by the changes in tide here; even at high tide with the large areas of sand covered, the shimmering blue waters can offer great potential. It's worth exploring at both high and low tide.

Opposite top: The incredible red rocks on the beach at Ardroil (VP1). Fujifilm X–T2, 14mm f/2.8, ISO 200, 6s at f/6.4. Sep.

The huge expanse of sand at low tide (VP1). Fujifilm X–T2, 18–55mm f/2.8–f/4, ISO 200, 400s at f/8. Sep.

Swirling sea around the red rocks of Ardroil. Fujifilm X–T2, 14mm f/2.8, ISO 200, 4.5s at f/6.4. Sep.

Looking along the dunes at Ardroil to Uig Lodge. Fujifilm X–T2, 14mm f/2.8, ISO 200, 1/12s at f/11. Sep.

Top left: layers of dunes and hills at Ardroil. Fujifilm X–T2, 55–200mm f/3.5–f/4.8, ISO 200, 1/125s at f/8. Sep. *Top right*: sheep in front to Uig Lodge. Fujifilm X–T2, 55–200mm f/3.5–f/4.8, ISO 200, 1/125s at f/8. Sep. *Above left*: the Lewis Chessman sculpture at Ardroil. Fujifilm X–T2, 18–55mm f/2.8–f/4, ISO 320, 1/550s at f/8. Sep. *Above right*: Rain sweeps across the hills to the south of the beach. Fujifilm X–T2, 18–55mm f/2.8–f/4, ISO 200, 0.6s at f/11. Sep.

8 UIG

Above: looking across the beach at high tide from the bouldery slopes above the dunes (VP1). Fujifilm X–T2, 18–55mm f/2.8–f/4, ISO 200, 1/10s at f/11. Sep. *Below*: textures in the rocks and sand at Ardroil.

Looking across one of the beaches on the Carnish Peninsula (VP2). Fujifilm X–T2, 18–55mm f/2.8–f/4, ISO 200, 1/280s at f/8. Sep.

Viewpoint 2 – Carnish Peninsula

At the western end of the bay, the Carnish peninsula juts out into the sea, separated from the main area of the beach by the Abhainn Dearg, the river which gives its name to the only whisky distillery in Lewis located just to the south. The obvious attraction here is the sandy bay which you arrive at first, however, heading around the peninsula reveals more hidden beaches and also gives a great outlook eastwards over Uig sands.

Sheep on the dunes at Carnish. Fujifilm X–T2, 55–200mm f/3.5–f/4.8, ISO 200, 1/1250s at f/3.5. Sep.

Another of the small sandy bays at Carnish. Fujifilm X–T2, 18–55mm f/2.8–f/4, ISO 200, 1/220s at f/9. Sep.

LEWIS – UIG   **101**

9 MANGERSTA

In contrast with the sedate and sheltered sands of Uig the coastline around Mangersta is a frenzied rush of pounding waves, jagged rock stacks and towering cliffs. It thrusts out into the Atlantic, catching the brunt of the Atlantic storms and can be an exhilarating place on a stormy day. On a clear day, the lucky visitor may even catch a glimpse of St Kilda on the horizon. Beyond that there is nothing but Atlantic ocean until you reach Newfoundland some 3000 kilometres to the west.

What to shoot and viewpoints

Viewpoint 1 – Mangersta Beach and Cliffs

Mangersta beach faces south west and attracts its fair share of wild waves. The best views are across the bay from the south towards the cliffs and rock outcrops, however, it is also worth exploring the dunes. Arguably the beach is best appreciated from above, with the cliffs on the southwest providing some nice vantage points for the onrushing waves. It is also worth exploring this flank as depending the tide some smaller sandy bays and pebble filled caves are revealed. The cliffs to the north are where this area gets very dramatic. A narrow path from the beach skirts the steep slope towards a cairn at the top of the cliff and provides a great view back across the beach and to the hills beyond. From here a wander along the clifftop paths takes you past huge cliffs, narrow chasms and tremendous rock buttresses above the turbulent waters. The colours of the cliffs here are fascinating with sunset in particular really emphasising the red striations in the rock. »

How to get here

From Uig, head south past Ardroil and cross the bridge at the distillery. Turn left and continue up the steep hill. Ignore the road on the right signposted to Mangersta and continue south west through an increasingly barren landscape. On passing a gate to the right you will notice a small parking area, set back on the left. On foot, follow the track down to the beach. To reach the stacks, continue on the road until a low brick building appears on the left, there is space for a car to park at the end of the track which leads to this building.

Viewpoint 1 – Mangersta Beach and Cliffs

- **Lat/Long:** 58.164022, -7.0821861
- **what3words:** ///sundial.stiff.escapades
- **Grid Ref:** NB012307
- **Postcode:** HS2 9EY

Above: the cliffs to the south west of Mangersta beach. Fujifilm X-T2, 55–200mm f/3.5–f/4.8, ISO 100, 1/40s at f/10. Sep.

Viewpoint 2 – Mangersta Stacks

- **Lat/Long:** 58.151256, -7.1003861
- **what3words:** ///timeless.hazelnuts.fishery
- **Grid Ref:** NB000293
- **Postcode:** HS2 9HA

Accessibility

Both viewpoints are close to the car parking areas, however, each involve clifftop walking. Whilst stormy weather is perfect for making dramatic images, these are dangerous places often with slippery grass above huge drops. A fall in these locations would be fatal so exercise caution particularly in high winds. The feint path to the shore at the stacks is loose and dangerous and probably not worth the risk.

Best time of year/day

Located on the west coast, these two viewpoints make ideal sunset locations. The stacks in particular are excellent at sunset, ideally coupled with a high tide and crashing waves.

Above: *looking across the beach at Mangersta as the waves rush out(VP1). Fujifilm X–T1, 18–55mm f/2.8–f/4, ISO 200, 2s at f/6.4. May.*
Below: *waves crashing against the cliffs at the north of the beach. Fujifilm X–T2, 55–200mm f/3.5–f/4.8, ISO 200, 1/170s at f/11. Sep.*

Above: the rock strewn headland of Aird Feinis. Fujifilm X–T2, 18–55mm f/2.8–f/4, ISO 200, 1/3s at f/8. Sep. *Opposite top*: the cliffs to the north of the Mangersta stacks (VP2), Fujifilm X–T1, 18–55mm f/2.8–f/4, ISO 200, 1/140s at f/6.4. May. *Opposite bottom*: rugged cliffs north of Mangersta beach. Fujifilm X–T2, 18–55mm f/2.8–f/4, ISO 200, 1/450s at f/8. Sep.

9 MANGERSTA

Viewpoint 2 – Mangersta Stacks

The coastline is at its most astounding slightly further south at the famous Mangersta Stacks. In a location where the sea is so powerful that coastal erosion could almost be a spectator sport, these dramatic pillars of rock stubbornly resist the battering waves. They are best seen from above along the headland at Aird Feinis. They can often be missed from the road, but a small hand painted sign along the road at NA 999 291 shows the way and faint paths lead you to the clifftop where the stacks are best photographed. On days of powerful swell the sight of the waves crashing against the stacks is simply awesome. It is possible to pick up a feint path down the steep cliffs to the bouldery shoreline, however, this route is not advisable. If you have time, the headland of Aird Feinis is also recommended. Some shapely boulders sit amongst dark pools and rocks veined with white quartz and the views from here are wide ranging with compositions to be found in all directions.

Top: Jagged rocky coastline to the south west of the beach. Fujifilm X–T2, 18–55mm f/2.8–f/4, ISO 200, 1/500s at f/6.4. Sep. **Middle**: Rain heading in from the west with the Flannan Isles on the horizon. Fujifilm X–T1, 18–55mm f/2.8–f/4, ISO 200, 1/170s at f/11. Sep. **Bottom**: the road to Mangersta. Fujifilm X–T2, 55–200mm f/3.5–f/4.8, ISO 200, 1/850s at f/6.4. Sep. **Below**: Rough sea at Mangersta beach. Fujifilm X–T2, 55–200mm f/3.5–f/4.8, ISO 200, 1/480s at f/10. May.

Top: side light on a boulder on Aird Feinis. Fujifilm X–T2, 18–55mm f/2.8–f/4, ISO 200, 1/4s at f/11. Sep. **Above**: the Mangersta Stacks. Fujifilm X–T2, 18–55mm f/2.8–f/4, ISO 200, 0.7s at f/11. Sep.

Above: chockstone on the cliffs north of Mangersta beach. Fujifilm X–T1, 18–55mm f/2.8–f/4, ISO 200, 1/500s at f/6.4. Sep. **Below**: cairn on Aird Feinis looking south with Harris in the distance, Fujifilm X–T2, 18–55mm f/2.8–f/4, ISO 200, 1/7s at f/8. Sep.

The Mangersta Stacks. Fujifilm X–T2, 18–55mm f/2.8–f/4, ISO 200, 7.5s at f/11. Sep.

HARRIS

HARRIS – INTRODUCTION

Of all the Hebridean islands, Harris is probably the one which I return to the most. There is something in particular about Harris, which to my mind, no other island has. It's a combination of the quality of the stark northern light, the complex layering of landscape and seascape and also a reassuring familiarity which draws me back time and time again. I find myself daydreaming about the ferry from Uig on Skye pulling into Tarbert, imagining the promontories of rock either side ushering me back to the island. Retracing the journey west over the rocky interior of the island with the view opening up towards Taransay across bands of shining sea. Thinking of that sudden reveal at Luskentyre as the dunes part and Traigh Rosamol blends from sand to sea to mountain.

The island itself is quite small by Hebridean standards but there is a variety of landscapes here which could occupy the photographer for a lifetime. The beaches of the west coast are unsurpassed in their beauty, a blend of white sand, turquoise seas and marram-clad dunes. There are many beaches in the Hebrides which possess such qualities, but none which feel quite as special as those on Harris. It really is like nowhere else. Then there is the southern coast of Harris with its intricately folded coastline of nooks and crannies where villages and houses sit nestled alongside small bays. Or there is mountainous North Harris, home to eagles and at the very westernmost end of the long road to Huisnis, yet more beautiful beaches.

Would I ever grow tired of watching the light on Luskentyre? Would I stop being amazed at the colours of the sky and sea at sunset? Would I get weary of the changeable weather, flinging hail a minute after sun?

Probably not, and I doubt you will either.

How to get to Harris

Ferry

You can catch a ferry to Stornoway, Lewis from Ullapool (2hrs 45m) then drive south to Harris, or save yourself some travel time and catch the ferry from Uig on Skye to Tarbert on Harris (2hrs 15m). If you are island hopping you can catch a ferry from Oban on the mainland to Barra (4hrs 45m) and drive north to Harris.

Air

It's an hour flight from Glasgow to either of the three island airports in the Outer Hebrides connecting the mainland to Stornoway Airport (Isle of Lewis), Benbecula Airport (Isle of Benbecula) and Barra Airport (Isle of Barra). Flights also leave Edinburgh and Inverness to the airports. Details at *loganair.co.uk*. You can rent a car on Barra, details at *carhire-hebrides.co.uk*

Previous spread: winter arrives on the North Harris Hills. Fujifilm X–T2, 55–200mm f/3.5–f/4.8, ISO 200, 13s at f/6.4. Feb.

HARRIS	
Scottish Gaelic	Na Hearadh.
Area	841 sq. miles (2178 sq. km).
Length/breadth	26 × 21 miles.
Highest Elevation	An Cliseam 799m (2,621 ft).
Owned by	North Harris Trust, private residents. Comhairle nan Eilean Siar, the Western Isles Council.
Population	1,916
Largest settlement(s)	Tarbet (pop. 550), Leverburgh (second biggest village), Hushinish (small hamlet), Northton (visitor's centre).
Vehicles allowed	Yes
Car/Bike rental	Harris Cycle Hire, Horgabost Bike Hire. Car hire: *carhire-hebrides.co.uk*
Public transport	Yes. Bus timetable at *cne-siar.gov.uk*
Day trips from mainland?	No
Internet/mobile phone coverage	Broadband. 3G/4G dependent on carrier. Poor or no reception away from main towns. Public wifi at ferry terminals.
Power	Grid and Wind.
Island website(s)	*explore-harris.com • visitouterhebrides.co.uk • visitscotland.com scotland.org.uk • undiscoveredscotland.co.uk*
Festivals/Events	Feis Mara na Hearadh (Isle of Harris Festival of the Sea in July). See more at *visitouterhebrides.co.uk/whats-on* and *hebevents.com*
Accommodation	Book well in advance for: camping, B&Bs and hostels, self catering, boutique hotels and spa-spec chalets. Book in advance at *explore-harris.com/accommodation*
Provisions/Eating Out	*explore-harris.com/eating-out • fir-chlis.co.uk/eating-out-in-harris orannamara.com/isle-of-harris-info/restaurants-isle-of-harris*
Wildlife	Otters, red deer, seals, dolphins, harbour porpoise and several species of whales. Redshank, greenshank, oystercatcher, curlew, ringed plover and dunlin. Shelduck and red-breasted Merganser (fish-eating duck) are to be seen on Loch Erisort, and large numbers of greylag geese and lapwing are found throughout the district.
Night Sky Bortle Scale	Class 1.

LOCATIONS

1. Luskentyre 116
2. Seilebost and Nisabost 130
3. Tràigh Iar and Mcleods Stone 142
4. Borve to Scarasta 148
5. Northton and Ceapabhal .. 156
6. Rodel and the Golden Road 164
7. North Harris 170
8. Scalpay 176

Maps

- OS Landranger Map 14 (1:50 000) Tarbert and Loch Seaforth

Overleaf: *Looking along Tràigh Rosamol to Ceapabhal. Fujifilm X–T2, 18–55mm f/2.8–f/4, ISO 200, 1/200s at f/6.4. Feb.*

1. LUSKENTYRE

The beaches at Luskentyre are arguably the most famous in the Hebrides, regularly gracing lists of the Top 10 beaches in the world. It's easy to see why, the combination of crystal clear waters and white sand alone would make a photographer jump for joy. However, it's more than that; there is a unique interplay at Luskentyre between sea, sky and mountains which is unsurpassed in Scotland. This is a location which can be returned to repeatedly, with an extravagance of photographic opportunities and one which the photographer will never tire of visiting. It is increasingly popular, however, once you visit you will understand why.

What to shoot and viewpoints

Viewpoint 1 – Road to Losgaintir ♿

The single track road to the village of Losgaintir winds its way along the coast, hugging the shoreline and offering a number of stopping points. The views here are mainly to the south and west across the tidal flats of Tràigh Losgaintir, however, a herd of Belted Galloway cows can provide some interest to the barren flanks of Beinn Losgaintir to the north. Depending on the level of the tide the view can be silvered slivers of water or a turquoise and blue shallow sea punctuated by sand bars. A good area for abstract studies of shape and colour, there are also some rocky headlands to provide foreground interest to wider shots. The tide moves quickly here so it's worth staying around and watching the changing view. »

How to get here

Luskentyre is accessed from the minor road which branches off the A859 at the bus stop. There are numerous stopping points along the road and a good sized car park at the cemetery where the road ends. The car park can get busy at times, please be careful not to park across access points. There is a public convenience in the car park.

Viewpoint 1 – Road to Losgaintir

- **Lat/Long:** 57.877631, -6.9297455
- **what3words:** ///dusted.corn.icebergs
- **Grid Ref:** NG078982
- **Postcode:** HS3 3HL

Viewpoint 2 – Tràigh Rosamol, Viewpoint 3 – Tràigh Rosamol Dunes & Viewpoint 4 – Headland

- **Lat/Long:** 57.891721, -6.9529780
- **what3words:** ///oldest.duck.headstone
- **Grid Ref:** NG066999
- **Postcode:** HS3 3HL

Top: stormy skies over the tidal flats and Taransay (VP1). Fujifilm X–T1, 18–55mm f/2.8–f/4, ISO 200, 1/210s at f/8. Mar.
Above: a road sign that always puts a smile on my face (VP1). Fujifilm X–T2, 55–200mm f/3.5–f/4.8, ISO 200, 1/480 at f/5.6. Feb.

Above: one of the rocky outcrops between the beach and the road (VP1). Fujifilm X–T2, 18–55mm f/2.8–f/4, ISO 200, 1/280s at f/11. Sep.
Below: The shifting patterns of water and sand (VP1). Fujifilm X–T2, 18–55mm f/2.8–f/4, ISO 200, 1/200s at f/11. Oct.

1 LUSKENTYRE

A wee boy sprints towards the sea (VP1). Fujifilm X–T2, 18–55mm f/2.8–f/4, ISO 200, 1/280s at f8. Jul.

1 LUSKENTYRE

The snow-capped Harris hills from the tideline along Tràigh Rosamol (VP2). Fujifilm X–T1, 18–55mm f/2.8–f/4, ISO 200, 1s at f/11. Jan.

Viewpoint 2 – Tràigh Rosamol

Tràigh Rosamol is accessed from the end of the road at the cemetery car park and is reached by a sandy track alongside a small stream. As you reach the end of this path, with dunes on your left and Beinn Losgaintir on your right, the beach opens up to reveal a fantastic vista; the hills of North Harris arrayed in front, the Isle of Taransay sheltering the beach and the turquoise sea along the shoreline. There are many opportunities here; if there is a big swell, the outrushing waves can provide a great foreground to the view north. The view south west to the distinctive hill of Ceapabhal works very well for a winter sunset. There is also potential in amongst the low dunes, looking to Beinn Losgaintir. Tràigh Rosamol is definitely a place to linger, savour and explore. »

The old Luskentyre cemetery. Fujifilm X–T2, 18–55mm f/2.8–f/4, ISO 200, 1/160s at f/8. Feb.

Opposite: moonset at Luskentyre. Fujifilm X–T2, 18–55mm f/2.8–f/4, ISO 200, 1.5s at f/11. Jun.

Next spread: reflections at Tràigh Rosamol (VP1). Fujifilm X–T2, 18–55mm f/2.8–f/4, ISO 200, 0.8s at f/11. Jun.

1 LUSKENTYRE

Accessibility
The viewpoints are all accessible from the road or good paths. Viewpoints 3 and 4 require some steep walking however nothing too taxing.

Next spread: winter dawn in the dunes at Tràigh Rosamol (VP3). Fujifilm X–T2, 18–55mm f/2.8–f/4, ISO 200, 1/15s at f/6.4. Feb.

Best time of year/day
This is a location which can work at any time. Under the blue skies of summer the beach takes on a tropical feel and in winter it can feel like a remote northern wind-lashed strand with wild waves crashing onto the shore. The colour of the sea over the shallow sand is a wonderful turquoise colour even under overcast skies so it offers photographic opportunities on days which might not otherwise appear promising. Tràigh Rosamol works well for both sunrise and sunset.

In amongst the dunes above Tràigh Rosamol. Fujifilm X–T2, 18–55mm f/2.8–f/4, ISO 200, 1/20s at f/8. Feb.

looking north from the high point of the dunes. Fujifilm X–T2, 14mm f/2.8, ISO 200, 1/17s at f/8. Feb.

Viewpoint 3 – Tràigh Rosamol Dunes

Ascending from the beach, the dunes begin to rise up, offering wonderful panoramic views of the Luskentyre area. From the highest dune the view to the North Harris hills and the Sound of Taransay is particularly special, however, there are images to be found in all directions from here. The marram grass makes an excellent foreground, especially on a windy day with a longer exposure to soften their form. >>

1 LUSKENTYRE

Looking down Tràigh Rosamol from the headland (VP4). Fujifilm X–T2, 18–55mm f/2.8–f/4, ISO 200, 1/75s at f/11. Oct.

Viewpoint 4 – Headland

To the north east of Tràigh Rosamol a finger of land extends out to the sea. Accessed by a gate to the north of the beach, a faint route along this headland leads to the remains of an old settlement. There are a number of interesting rocky coves along here and some geological forms which provide great foreground interest to the view north. Beinn Losgaintir looks particularly dramatic from here, with a precipitous slope leading to the waters of Loch a Siar

*Opposite top: the view up West Loch Tarbert from the end of the headland. Fujifilm X–T2, 18–55mm f/2.8–f/4, ISO 200, 1/300s at f/8. Oct. **Bottom**: precariously balanced boulder (VP4). Fujifilm X–T2, 18–55mm f/2.8–f/4, ISO 200, 1/450s at f/8. Oct.*

Rain approaching the rocky shoreline on the headland (VP4). Fujifilm X–T2, 18–55mm f/2.8–f/4, ISO 200, 1/450s at f/8. Oct.

2 SEILEBOST AND NISABOST

The beach at Seilebost will be familiar to you if you have already visited Luskentyre as it forms the southern part of this great bay, tantalisingly close but separated at low tide by a meandering river. North facing, the beach looks directly towards Tràigh Rosamol and the North Harris hills. Nisabost (also known as Horgabost) is a little further to the west, and will be right on your doorstep if you decide to camp at the site behind the beach.

What to shoot and viewpoints

Viewpoint 1 – Seilebost Beach
The beach is accessed easily from the car park, with a gentle stroll over the machair. As the feint path rises up to the largest dune, the beach is revealed to the north. It's a fantastic sight, a curving spit of sand heading north towards Luskentyre and the North Harris Hills backed by flowing dunes and marram grass. There are numerous compositions to be made both here and at the beach

How to get here
From Tarbert head south on the A859 which climbs through the rocky landscape. After 10 minutes you will begin descending on a swooping road down towards the west with tantalising glimpses of Luskentyre and Taransay. Continue on over the causeway and after a bend look out for the Seilebost School sign which directs you to the right. A minor road leads to a small parking area outside the old school. The lay-by in Viewpoint 2 is just a minute further on along the A859. Nisabost beach is accessed through the campsite at Horgabost.

Viewpoint 1 – Seilebost Beach
Lat/Long:	57.868653, -6.9532361
what3words:	///beanbag.lease.streak
Grid Ref:	NG063973
Postcode:	HS3 3HP

Viewpoint 2 – Seilebost Viewpoint
Lat/Long:	57.867294, -6.9655306
what3words:	///kingpin.standards.after
Grid Ref:	NG056972
Postcode:	HS3 3HR

Viewpoint 3 – Nisabost
Lat/Long:	57.86324, -6.9802944
what3words:	///change.joined.handyman
Grid Ref:	NG047968
Postcode:	HS3 3HR

Accessibility
Accessibility couldn't be easier. Viewpoint 1 requires a short stroll across the dunes and scramble down them to access the beach. Viewpoint 2, essentially you just have to open your car door. Viewpoint 3 starts when you leave the car park.

Best time of year/day
North facing, these viewpoints work at both sunset and sunrise, however, Seilebost beach is best at dawn as the sun illuminates the marram grass particularly well. Viewpoint 2 is worth visiting as you pass, at anytime; if the weather is particularly changeable it is a good spot to wait safe and dry in the car for some post-storm light. Nisabost is an ideal location if you are camping at the site, but is also worth visiting in its own right. If you are pushed for time, Seilebost is the best dawn location. There are images to be made at all times of the year, even in the height of summer the wonderful colours of the water can't fail to excite the most reluctant of daytime photographers.

Above: Ridges in the sand at sunrise on the beach at Seilebost (VP1). Fujifilm X–T1, 18–55mm f/2.8–f/4, ISO 200, 0.5s at f/8. Mar.

Next spread: The crystal clear waters at Seilebost. Fujifilm X–T1, 18–55mm f/2.8–f/4, ISO 200, 1/125s at f/8. Jul.

Above: looking across to Luskentyre from the Seilebost dunes. Fujifilm X–T2, 55–200mm f/3.5–f/4.8, ISO 200, 1/180 at f/8. Jul.
Below: a winter dawn at Seilebost (VP1). Fujifilm X–T1, 14mm f/2.8, ISO 200, 1/3s at f/8. Jan.

SEILEBOST AND NISABOST

side base of the dunes. This landscape changes often, with winter storms depositing sand or blowing out areas of dunes so, you never quite know what to expect. It is a must-visit location, and one which will inspire any photographer. The beach itself offers more opportunities and it is worth walking to the end of the sand before returning on the eastern side of the beach. In summer in particular, the colour of the shallow waters is breathtaking.

Viewpoint 2 – Seilebost Viewpoint ♿

As the road rises up to a high point on the cliffs to the south west, there is a large lay-by on the right hand side and it offers quite possibly the greatest roadside view in Scotland. A stunning panorama encompassing Seilebost, Taransay, Luskentyre and the North Harris Hills with the sinuous river snaking across the sand of the bay, with some of the most intense blues you will see anywhere. Even under cloud the sea seams to glow with a pale luminescence like it is being lit from below. It's hard not to stop at it every time you pass and it is worth spending some time here, especially in changing weather conditions as the play of light on the sea is very special. This location also offers some great potential for telephoto work, by using a long lens to isolate patterns in the tidal areas between the outflow of the river and the edge of the sea. »

Along the dunes at Seilebost. Fujifilm X–T2, 18–55mm f/2.8–f/4, ISO 200, 1/300s at f/8. Feb.

Top left: Number 1 Luskentyre from the Seilebost viewpoint (VP2). Fujifilm X–T1, 55–200mm f/3.5–f/4.8, ISO 200, 1/350 at f/16. Mar. **Right**: Paddle-boarding at Nisabost (VP3). Fujifilm X–T2, 55–200mm f/3.5–f/4.8, ISO 200, 1/180 at f/4. Jul.

Above: Big skies above the north Harris Hills (VP2). Fujifilm X–T2, 14mm f/2.8, ISO 200, 1/600s at f/8. Jul.

Left: Patterns in the sea and sand as seen from the Seilebost Viewpoint (VP2). Fujifilm X–T1, 55–200mm f/3.5–f/4.8, ISO 200, 1/350 at f/10. Mar

Opposite top left: Summer in the dunes at Seilebost. Fujifilm X–T2, 18–55mm f/2.8–f/4, ISO 200, 1/125s at f/8. Jul.
Bottom right: Sand detail at Nisabost (VP3). Fujifilm X–T2, 18–55mm f/2.8–f/4, ISO 200, 1/5s at f/8. Jul.

SEILEBOST AND NISABOST

The best view from a lay-by anywhere? (VP2). Fujifilm X–T2, 14mm f/2.8, ISO 200, 1/450s at f/8. Jul.

2 SEILEBOST AND NISABOST

Number 1 Luskentyre through the machair from Nisabost. Fujifilm X–T2, 55–200mm f/3.5–f/4.8, ISO 200, 1/2200 at f/4. Jul.

Viewpoint 3 – Nisabost

Nisabost beach is not as dramatic as Seilebost beach, but it still has much to offer the photographer, especially if you happen to be camping beside it. The view north is as equally appealing as Seilebost, and at the eastern end there are some interesting rock formations which can form good foregrounds. The beach has a more sheltered, intimate feel to others on Harris, surrounded as it is by Luskentyre, North Harris and Taransay and without a view of an open Atlantic horizon.

Sunset from the dunes at Nisabost. Fujifilm X–T2, 14mm f/2.8, ISO 200, 1/75s at f/8. Jul.

Summer evening on the beach at Nisabost. Fujifilm X–T2, 18–55mm f/2.8–f/4, ISO 200, 0.8s at f/11. Jul.

3 TRÀIGH IAR AND MCLEOD'S STONE

This stretch of coast from Tràigh Iar south to Borve is a veritable treasure trove for seascape photography. There are sandy beaches which attract big waves and surfers, rocky headlands with coves to be explored and an ancient megalith perched on a hillside. Always worth a visit (or two) is Talla na Mara, the community enterprise centre run by The West Harris Trust; a fabulous building which houses their headquarters, artists studios, a restaurant and a gallery space.

The rocky shore of Tràigh Iar looking to Ceapabhal (VP1). Fujifilm X–T2, 14mm f/2.8, ISO 200, 6s at f/11. Oct.

What to shoot and viewpoints

Viewpoint 1 – Tràigh Iar

As its name suggests this beach faces west (Iar) and as such it attracts a big swell which seems to rush in between Ceapabhal and Taransay before crashing on the sand. Often poplar with surfers, it offers a lot of opportunity for the photographer, from the wide view north along the beach with Mcleod's Stone perched on the hillside to the wave-worn rock formations at the northern and southern tips. The dark metamorphic rock shot through with colourful strata at the northern end of the beach are particularly interesting. The possibilities here vary with the level of the tide so it is worth exploring on a few different occasions. »

How to get here

From Tarbert head south on the A859 which climbs through the rocky landscape. After 10 minutes you will begin descending on a swooping road down towards the west with tantalising glimpses of Luskentyre and Taransay. After passing the campsite at Horgabost the road rises up to a cattle grid before heading down towards Tràigh Iar and there is a lay-by on the right. From here head through the gate to the beach. To reach the stone head north to the end of the beach and pick your way up the dunes. The stone will come into view again as you ascend the slope. For Viewpoints 3 and 4 park in the small lay-by on the right hand side of the road to the south of Talla na Mara. From this point you can explore to the coastline to the north as well as picking your way along the coast south as far as Borve. There are no tracks for this section, however, it is easy enough to find your way.

Viewpoint 1 – Tràigh Iar & Viewpoint 2 – Mcleod's Stone

- **Lat/Long:** 57.859519, -6.9937583
- **what3words:** ///notifying.twist.leaflet
- **Grid Ref:** NG039964
- **Postcode:** HS3 3HR

Viewpoint 3 – Rocky shoreline & Viewpoint 4 – Borve

- **Lat/Long:** 57.854731, -7.0000222
- **what3words:** ///cabbages.peddling.surer
- **Grid Ref:** NG035959
- **Postcode:** HS3 3HT

Accessibility

Viewpoint 1 is essentially roadside. Viewpoint 2 requires a short climb up a steep slope but nothing too taxing. Viewpoints 3 and 4 are along a rocky coastline which is pathless and sometimes above rough seas. Care needs to be taken in stormy conditions.

Best time of year/day

Tràigh Iar is classic sunset location; west facing it catches the last light of the day and the spray from the breakers shimmers in the low sun. The rest of the coastline works well at sunset, however, there is plenty of intrigue provided by the geology on days of flat light. McLeod's stone works in most conditions, but if you happen to the there at the equinox, make sure you look for St Kilda on the horizon at sunset.

Above: outrushing waves at Tràigh Iar. Fujifilm X–T1, 14mm f/2.8, ISO 200, 0.7s at f/11. Feb. **Below**: Ancient wave-smoothed rock at the north of Tràigh Iar. Fujifilm X–T2, 14mm f/2.8, ISO 200, 422s at f/11. Feb.

3 TRÀIGH IAR AND MCLEOD'S STONE

The view from above McLeod's Stone towards Talla na Mara. Fujifilm X–T2, 18–55mm f/2.8–f/4, ISO 200, 1/18s at f/11. Jul.

Viewpoint 2 – Mcleod's Stone
Roughly 5000 years ago, Mcleod's Stone (Clach Mhic Leòid) was erected on the slopes above Tràigh Iar. Over 2m in height and leaning at a precarious angle it gazes out to the Atlantic, bearing witness to many changes in land, sea and population over its long history. At the equinoxes the sun sets over St Kilda from the stone, perhaps a hint to the long forgotten reasons behind its creation? Whilst there isn't much for foreground interest, the stone itself provides a point of intrigue in the view across to Taransay or along the west coast of Harris and is a grand place to watch the clouds race in off the Atlantic.

Viewpoint 3 – Rocky shoreline
To the south of Tràigh Iar the shoreline becomes increasingly more fractured and rocky with a number of inlets pushing inland. Perhaps not as initially appealing as some other stretches of the Harris coastline, this area has its own charms and there are number of interesting rock formations and smaller coves which deserve to be explored on the way to the next beach at Borve. »

Macleod's Stone with Taransay beyond (VP2). Fujifilm X–T1, 14mm f/2.8, ISO 200, 4.5s at f/11. Mar.

3 TRÀIGH IAR AND MCLEOD'S STONE

Looking across to Ceapabhal from the rocky shoreline south of Tràigh Iar. Fujifilm X–T2, 14mm f/2.8, ISO 200, 28s at f/11. Oct.

Viewpoint 4 – Borve

The beach at Borve is less popular, perhaps due to the lack of direct access from the road, but is definitely worth visiting if you have walked south as described in Viewpoint 3. A stile gives access over the fence and across a smaller pebble beach before opening out onto a sandy bay edged with some interesting black and red rock outcrops, a perfect foil for the white sand. At low tide it is also possible to walk around onto a further sandy bay.

Weathered rocks to the south of Tràigh Iar. Fujifilm X–T2, 18–55mm f/2.8–f/4, ISO 200, 1/18s at f/8. Oct

Opposite: *Sunset at Borve. Fujifilm X–T2, 18–55mm f/2.8–f/4, ISO 200, 8.5s at f/11. Oct.*

Above: Waves of rock and sea at Borve. Fujifilm X–T2, 18–55mm f/2.8–f/4, ISO 200, 1/900s at f/8. Oct.

4 BORVE TO SCARASTA

Driving along the Atlantic coast is one of the great journeys in Scotland. Around every corner there is another beautiful scene and the urge to stop is hard to ignore. As you crest the steep road to the top of the golf course you catch your first glimpse of the beach at Scarista, it's a dramatic view in any conditions, but with the swell up and the breakers racing onto shore it is hard to beat. Within this location there are three beaches, each with their own character and all offer a wealth of possibilities for the seascape photographer.

Swooshery at Bàgh Steinigidh (VP1), Fujifilm X–T2, 10–24mm f/4, ISO 200, 4s at f/5.6. Oct.

What to shoot and viewpoints

Viewpoint 1 – Bàgh Steinigidh

This fine beach is easily missed as you drive along the coastal road. It is small, steeply sloping and overlooked by two houses; it doesn't exactly stand out as one of the most interesting beaches to photograph on Harris. But it definitely is! For some reason, perhaps the steeply sloping nature of the sand and the black rock outcrops it catches some really powerful waves and this makes for some very interesting seascapes. Also known as the Bay of Soaking Wellies, the unpredictable nature of the waves here can lead to some very wet socks, luckily the car park is right beside the beach! The rock outcrops here make the perfect foil for long exposures as the waves race out. »

Opposite: a relatively calm moment at Bàgh Steinigidh, Fujifilm X–T2, 10–24mm f/4, ISO 200, 26s at f/8. Oct.

How to get here

All of these viewpoints are located on the A859, the main road which runs down the west coast of Harris. As you pass through the village of Borve, passing Scarista post office look out for a small car park on the right hand side beside a large house. This gives direct access to Bàgh Steinigidh. To reach Tràigh Mhòr walk back up the main road and pass through the first gate on the left. Cross the field aiming for the far north western corner where a gate gives access to the beach. To reach Tràigh Scarasta, there is a small lay-by beside the graveyard of Scarista Church which can accommodate a vehicle or two. Walk back up the road until you reach the first house on the left. A gate gives access to to the grazing land and a path takes you across to the dunes.

Viewpoint 1 – Bàgh Steinigidh & Viewpoint 2 – Tràigh Mhòr

- Lat/Long: 57.834172, -7.0242889
- what3words: ///masking.named.adverbs
- Grid Ref: NG019938
- Postcode: HS3 3HX

Viewpoint 3 – Tràigh Scarasta

- Lat/Long: 57.825344, -7.0433278
- what3words: ///sparkles.jammy.study
- Grid Ref: NG007929
- Postcode: HS3 3HX

Accessibility

Viewpoint 1 is essentially roadside, however, the beach is steeply sloping and the waves are both powerful and unpredictable. Rocks which previously seem to be above the tide suddenly get swamped. Viewpoint 2 is a short 10 minutes walk across a field and then along the beach. The dunes can be steep but are not essential. Viewpoints 3 is easily accessed and the walk along the beach can really be as short or as long as you like.

Best time of year/day

These three viewpoints are best visited at sunset. However, don't discount them at other times either, there is enough potential here to make images in all but the very worst of conditions. If there is a big swell the breakers at Tràigh Scarasta are fantastic and if you get he combination of big waves and sunset conditions it can be magical. The machair is in bloom from May until fading out towards the end of August.

4 BORVE TO SCARASTA

Tendrils in the sand at Tràigh Mhòr (VP2). Fujifilm X–T1, 14mm f/2.8, ISO 200, 1/340s at f/8. Mar.

Viewpoint 2 – Tràigh Mhòr

Tràigh Mhòr (Big Beach) is also known as Borve beach and is another fine bay on the west coast of Harris. The beach is accessed through a field which contains a solitary standing stone, the last remnant of an ancient stone circle, a worthy subject. The beach is most interesting at the south western end where there is an excellent contrast between the black rocks and the yellow sand. The large dunes to the east are also worth scrambling up as they provide a fine vantage point for the view north, as well as catching the evening sun beautifully. »

Previous spread: *Outgoing tide at Bàgh Steinigidh. Fujifilm X–T1, 14mm f/2.8, ISO 200, 2s at f/9. Mar.*

Looking across to Taransay from the south of Tràigh Mhòr. Fujifilm X–T1, 14mm f/2.8, ISO 200, 20s at f/11. Dec.

The standing stone on the way to Tràigh Mhòr (VP2).

4 BORVE TO SCARASTA

Top left: Red House at Scarasta (VP3). Fujifilm X–E1, 18–55mm f/2.8–f/4, ISO 200, 1/110s at f/16. Jul. **Top Right**: *crofthouse behind Sgarasta beach. Fujifilm X–T2, 55–200mm f/3.5–f/4.8, ISO 200, 1/600 at f/11. Sep.* **Above left**: *the grazing land at Sgarasta. Fujifilm X–T1, 55–200mm f/3.5–f/4.8, ISO 200, 1/1170 at f/8. Jan.* **Above Right**: *geese with remnants of lazy beds behind. Fujifilm X–T2, 55–200mm f/3.5–f/4.8, ISO 200, 1/1500 at f/4.5. Sep.*

Viewpoint 3 – Tràigh Scarasta

Of all the beaches in Harris, Tràigh Scarasta might just be the most dramatic. Loomed over by the distinctive hill of Ceapabhal its 2 mile long shore can either be a delight to walk along or a challenge if the wind is up. Either way it is well worth exploring the whole beach and the dunes behind. It is bisected to the north by a stream which cuts a steep channel through the sand before fanning out

Top: ragged clouds over Ceapabhal (VP3). Fujifilm X–T1, 18–55mm f/2.8–f/4, ISO 200, 5s at f/10. Apr. **Above left**: Along the tideline on Tràigh Scarasta. Fujifilm X–T1, 14mm f/2.8, ISO 400, 6s at f/10. Mar. **Above Right**: Looking south along Tràigh Scarasta from the rocky headland at the north of the beach. Fujifilm X–T1, 18–55mm f/2.8–f/4, ISO 200, 1/3s at f/10. Apr.

along the waterside; this offers many possibilities for foregrounds. To the north the rocky headland provides a counterpoint to the sand and also provides views back up the west coast. The machair at Scarista is one of the most beautiful examples in Harris, and in spring and summer the profusion of wildflowers is incredible.

5 NORTHTON AND CEAPABHAL

The diminutive hill of Ceapabhal appears in so many images taken on the west coast of Harris with its distinctive rolling profile and flash of feldspar running across the flank. It certainly makes a great subject but it is also a fine viewpoint in itself, providing incredible views in all directions. There are numerous other attractions in this area of Harris including the salt marsh at Northton, yet more deserted beaches and even a ruined temple sitting above a remote sandy bay.

hopping over the first couple of channels which lead you onto the marsh as the elegant channels cut through the marsh provide fantastic lead in lines to Ceapabhal. »

What to shoot and viewpoints

Viewpoint 1 – Northton Salt Marsh

Tràigh Scarasta bites deeply into the land, almost turning Toe Head and Ceapabhal into a peninsula. It is covered at high tide by shallow water making it an ideal habitat for wading birds such lapwing, plover and oystercatcher. At the south western end it becomes a salt marsh, a complex network of flowing channels, sinuous pools and tussocky islands. Viewed from the road it is an interesting landscape, however, it is best experienced from from the marsh itself. It is definitely worth donning wellies or

How to get here

The village of Northton is located at the southwestern end of Harris, just as the A859 turns south east toward Leverburgh. As you pass through the village, keep your eyes open for Croft 36 on the right, an honesty shop offering lovely baked goods and meals. Further on is the Temple Cafe serving great coffee and cakes; you are spoilt for choice in Northton! There is small area for parking at the end of the road, however, be sure not to block any access point or turning area. The beach is accessed up the road to the left as you face Ceapabhal. There is a track along the edge of the beach which leads onto the headland and around to Tràigh na h-Uidhe. Viewpoint 1 is reached from the A859 before the turn-off to Northton, with a small parking bay off the road at an area of woodland, from there walk north along the road and after the third passing place head down the bank, keeping your eyes peeled for the submerged stepping stones.

Viewpoint 1 – Northton Salt Marsh

- **Lat/Long:** 57.795525, -7.0587167
- **what3words:** ///regret.ruling.mixer
- **Grid Ref:** NF995896
- **Postcode:** HS3 3JA

Viewpoint 2 – Temple and beaches & Viewpoint 3 – Ceapabhal

- **Lat/Long:** 57.801575, -7.073217
- **what3words:** ///codes.screamed.scribbled
- **Grid Ref:** NF987904
- **Postcode:** HS3 3JA

Accessibility

The best views of the salt marsh in Viewpoint 1 are reached via a short scramble down a steep bank from the road and involves either wading across the channels or hopping over on the submerged stepping stones. Be careful as the muddy bottom of the channels can be very soft. The walk out to the temple is relatively flat and easy, with paths along most of the way. Ceapabhal is very steep and pathless and requires care, particulary on the descent.

Best time of year/day

The salt marsh works well in most conditions and is a useful location to visit outside of the golden hours. The walk along the beaches is great in the evening, being west facing they are excellent sunset locations. Ceapabhal is worth climbing at any time, although a day of clear visibility is recommended, especially if you are hoping to catch a glimpse of the elusive St Kilda.

Sinuous curves in the salt marsh. Fujifilm X–T2, 55–200mm f/3.5–f/4.8, ISO 200, 1/160 at f/6.4. Sep.

Looking down on the salt marsh from the road. Fujifilm X–T2, 18–55mm f/2.8–f/4, ISO 200, 1/120s at f/8. Sep.

Opposite: the view from the marsh looking to Ceapabhal. Fujifilm X–T2, 18–55mm f/2.8–f/4, ISO 200, 120s at f/8. Sep.

5 NORTHTON AND CEAPABHAL

Along the headland across the lazy beds to Ceapabhal. Fujifilm X–T1, 14mm f/2.8, ISO 200, 1/600s at f/8. Mar.

Viewpoint 2 – Temple and beaches

The approach to Ceapabhal is one of the best coastal walks in Harris. Starting at Tràigh na h-Uidhe, itself a delightful sandy beach with an outlook towards Pabbay and Berneray, a cliff top path heads around the headland to the north. Along this section of headland you will notice the unique undulations in the land creating an almost corrugated impression. These are the remnants of 'lazy beds', a method of arable cultivation which was once ubiquitous in the Hebrides whereby peat was lifted in long trenches and mixed with seaweed to provide a fertile growing medium. The channels formed by removing the soil then became the drainage routes, taking excess water away from the crops. They are particularly evident when the sun is low, appearing as sinuous parallel shadows across hillsides throughout the Hebrides. Once past the lazy beds a series of beaches come into view with the temple perched out at the end. All the beaches have their charms, however, the main attraction is Rubh' an Teampaill, a 15th century chapel located in an incredibly picturesque

Rubh' an Teampaill. Fujifilm X–T2, 18–55mm f/2.8–f/4, ISO 200, 1/400s at f/8. Feb.

setting above the final sandy bay. It sits on the location of an Iron Age broch, however, archaeologists believe that the area has been in use for over 9000 years.

Tràigh na h-Uidhe with Pabbay on the horizon. Fujifilm X–T1, 14mm f/2.8, ISO 200, 1/2200s at f/7.1. Mar.

Rubh' an Teampaill from the dunes. Fujifilm X–T2, 18–55mm f/2.8–f/4, ISO 200, 1/210s at f/8. Feb.

Viewpoint 3 – Ceapabhal

From Tràigh na Cleabhaig, Ceapabhal looks incredibly steep, looming above to the north west. It is steep and boggy and the lower areas are pathless, but if you want a fantastic view it is well worth the effort. Head up from the beach in a north westerly direction and pick your way through the rocks and heather, there are some sheep tracks that can be followed. As height is gained the views behind you really start to open up. The many small islands scattered in the Sound of Harris with Berneray and North Hills beyond is a lovely sight. On reaching the broad summit the views to the north east open up and they are jaw dropping; all the beaches on the west of Harris strung out along the coast, one after another of beautiful jewels surrounded by turquoise seas. To the north, the Harris hills tower on the horizon, and in front of them, the island of Taransay sits just off shore, uninhabited since the days

5 NORTHTON AND CEAPABHAL

Panorama from the summit of Ceapabhal looking up the west coast of Harris. Fujifilm X–T1, 55–200mm f/3.5–f/4.8, ISO 200, 1/400 at f/10. Mar.

of Ben Fogle and his fellow TV Castaways. Almost due west on the horizon is St Kilda which can be glimpsed on those clear days. If you are visiting in summer on your return to Tràigh na Cleabhaig bear west across the dunes and pick up the path which leads through the machair, the colours and diversity of species is fantastic.

The many isles in the Sound of Harris from Ceapabhal. Fujifilm X–T2, 55–200mm f/3.5–f/4.8, ISO 200, 1/420 at f/8. Mar.

Opposite: *Machair at Northton. Fujifilm X–T2, 55–200mm f/3.5–f/4.8, ISO 200, 1/640 at f/3.5. Sep.*

[5] NORTHTON AND CEAPABHAL

A sheep poses for scale in the view across the Sound of Harris from the top of Ceapabhal. Fujifilm X–T1, 14mm f/2.8, ISO 200, 1/1600s at f/8. Mar.

6 RODEL AND THE GOLDEN ROAD

There could not be a bigger contrast between the two sides of Harris. Gone are the sweeping sands of Luskentyre and Scarista replaced by an altogether more barren, rocky and desolate landscape which looks out towards the north of Skye. With huge expanses of smooth grey weather worn rock, peppered with isolated boulders, it is often described as a 'moonscape' and was actually used to represent Jupiter in Kubrick's 2001: A Space Odyssey. The coastline in this area of south east of Harris is incredibly intricate with countless tiny bays and inlets along its frayed edge. Small villages or lone houses perch out on the rocks or huddle into sheltered coves and the photographic potential really is endless. Otters are common here and seals can often be seen in the bays, so a long lens may come in handy for any chance encounters.

Also know as the Bays of Harris, the area was settled by the victims of forced evictions from the fertile lands on the west coast. Relocated to provide land for sheep grazing, these people were forced to the very edge of the island on a harsh coast where the soil lies thin over the bedrock of the earth. One can only imagine the difficulty they had in attempting to scratch a living out of this environment. The land is so unforgiving that they even carried their dead over a pass (the Coffin Road) to the softer earth on the west coast in order to give them a burial.

These disparate settlements were once linked by the sea, however, are now joined by The Golden Road, apparently named on account of how much it cost to construct. This sinuous single track road will either excite or terrify the driver, with blind summits, sharp corners and twists and turns all along its 20 mile length. However, it is essential (perhaps as a passenger!) to experience the other side of Harris. It is best travelled in a north eastwards direction as this keeps the sun out of your eyes.

What to shoot and viewpoints

Viewpoint 1 – Rodel

Before undertaking the Golden Road, there is plenty to attract the photographer at Rodel, the church of St Clements being the obvious draw. It's a grand medieval building in a beautiful location with views across the Minch to Skye. It can be photographed from a number of locations, the small rise to the east of the road gives a good vantage point. Look out for the heart and star shaped rocks set within the boundary wall of the graveyard. While you are here it is worth walking the loop road which drops down to a small harbour at the Rodel Hotel which is currently being refurbished. There is an unusual grass topped pier and often a few boats bobbing in the water. »

Opposite: the path to St Clements Church at Rodel (VP1). Fujifilm X–T2, 10–24mm f/4, ISO 200, 1/4000s at f/8. Oct.

How to get here

From Leverburgh head south on the A859 for 2.6 miles, as you reach the church there is small parking area on the right at a cattle grid. Beyond the church the road heads continues on to Finsbay.

Rodel and the start of the Golden Road

- **Lat/Long**: 57.741139, -6.9623000
- **what3words**: ///note.fuse.crusaders
- **Grid Ref**: NG048832
- **Postcode**: HS5 3TW is 0.765 km from NG048832

Map

OS Landranger Map 14 (1:50 000) Tarbert and Loch Seaforth.

Accessibility

Rodel is essentially roadside with a short walk along a minor road to reach the harbour or a stroll up the hill to the north. Along the Golden Road parking spots are limited, so some of the views you notice from the car may require walking back along the road after finding a suitable place to stop. Be courteous and avoid blocking any entrances. There are some larger passing places which can facilitate a quick 'run and gun' style of shooting.

Best time of year/day

The bays are east facing and are an ideal location for sunrise, but they are also fantastic at sunset when the name the Golden Road may take on a new connotation. In winter the harshness of the land is emphasised and in summer the flowering lilies in the lochans provide some lovely softness to the austere landscape.

Top: stripy sheep at Rodel. Fujifilm X–T2, 55–200mm f/3.5–f/4.8, ISO 200, 1/1000 at f/4.5. Jul. **Middle**: Fionnsbhagh sign. Fujifilm X–T2, 10–24mm f/4, ISO 200, 1/200s at f/8. Oct. **Bottom**: heart of stone in the boundary wall of St Clements. Fujifilm X–T2, 18–55mm f/2.8–f/4, ISO 200, 1/150s at f/3.6. Sep.

St Clements from the hillside east of the road. Fujifilm X–T2, 10–24mm f/4, ISO 200, 1/170s at f/8. Oct.

RODEL AND THE GOLDEN ROAD

6 RODEL AND THE GOLDEN ROAD

Cottage at Manish reflected in Ob Leasaid (VP3). Fujifilm X–T2, 18–55mm f/2.8–f/4, ISO 200, 1/160s at f/7.1. Mar.

THE GOLDEN ROAD

Viewpoint 2 – Rodel to Finsbay ♿

As you leave Rodel, the road heads around a bend and the view out across the Minch really opens up. A favoured location for whale watchers, there are a number of lay-bys along this stretch of road which afford good look out spots. The road turns inland and the land becomes more rocky and grey, with boulders poking through heather. The road gradually descends to the village of Finsbay and a small parking area on the right provides a spot to stop and catch your breath. In the village of Finsbay be sure to visit the fantastic Mission House Gallery to see the work of sculptor Nikolai Globe and photographer Beka Globe. »

One of many still lochans beside the road. Fujifilm X–T2, 18–55mm f/2.8–f/4, ISO 200, 1/320s at f/8. Mar.

Top right: the winding road across the rocky landscape. Fujifilm X–T2, 18–55mm f/2.8–f/4, ISO 200, 1/200s at f/8. Mar.

Looking south across a lochan to Skye. Fujifilm X–T2, 18–55mm f/2.8–f/4, ISO 200, 1/150s at f/8. Mar.

6 RODEL AND THE GOLDEN ROAD

The view over Manish to Skye. Fujifilm X–T2, 18–55mm f/2.8–f/4, ISO 200, 1/180s at f/8. Mar.

Viewpoint 3 – Finsbay to the North ♿

From Finsbay onwards the land becomes more settled, with small villages and clusters of houses secreted away in the small bays. There will be numerous photographic possibilities which will catch your eye as you drive along and it is worth also exploring some of the smaller roads which branch off on the seaward side. Of particular interest is the view across Manish to the sheltered natural harbour of Ob Leasaid. A small building known as The Old Post Office, sits beside the water with its red roof gradually rusting away and it makes a fascinating subject in the wider view. At Aird Mhige, is possible to deviate back to the A859, however, it is worth carrying on along the coast, through the villages of Cluer, Grosebay and Scadabay, especially in summer when the lochans are full of flowering lillies. Once you arrive at the A859, if you are heading back towards the west coast it is worth stopping at the small parking area 500m south of the Grosebay turn off. It affords a lovely view south towards the Bays.

__Opposite left__: an old croft house at Manish. Fujifilm X–T2, 18–55mm f/2.8–f/4, ISO 200, 1/80s at f/10. May. __Opposite top__: red-roofed house at Geocrab. Fujifilm X–T2, 18–55mm f/2.8–f/4, ISO 200, 1/250s at f/10. Mar. __Opposite bottom__: sailing past The Bays of Harris. Fujifilm X–T2, 18–55mm f/2.8–f/4, ISO 200, 1/1500s at f/8. Jul

Top left: lilies in a lochan at the northern end of the Golden Road. Fujifilm X–T2, 18–55mm f/2.8–f/4, ISO 200, 1/100s at f/8. Jul.
Top middle: a landscape of bog and boulders. Fujifilm X–T2, 18–55mm f/2.8–f/4, ISO 200, 1/250s at f/8. Sep. **Top right**: abandoned crofthouse, Fujifilm X–E1, 18–55mm f/2.8–f/4, ISO 200, 1/60s at f/8. Jul. **Middle left**: lilies in a lochan at Grosebay. Fujifilm X–E1, 18–55mm f/2.8–f/4, ISO 200, 1/250s at f/8. Jul. **Middle right**: the chimneys of the Rodel Hotel with Skye beyond. Fujifilm X–T2, 55–200mm f/3.5–f/4.8, ISO 200, 1/1000 at f/4.8. Sep.

7. NORTH HARRIS

The north of Harris is less visited than both the fantastic beaches of the west coast and the golden road. It is a stark landscape, with foreboding peaks looming over a lonely single track road which twists and turns over hills and alongside lochs. The road passes isolated settlements, a dramatic castle and what may be the most remote tennis court in Scotland. It eventually reaches Huishnish, and hidden beyond is one of the Hebrides most attractive beaches, sheltered from the Atlantic by the island of Scarp.

What to shoot and viewpoints

Viewpoint 1 – The road to Hùisinis ♿

There are numerous moments of interest along the road to Hùisinis and you will often feel the need to stop and explore. The first is the old whaling station at Bunavoneader, with a red brick chimney and few ruins being all that remains of a once important local industry. Car parking spaces are rare along this road, however, there are some larger passing places where a car can be accommodated for a quick roadside shot. Of particular interest to wildlife photographers is the Eagle Observatory which is located in Glean Meavaig and is reached via a 2km walk from the road. The building is towered over by some dramatic rock buttresses and these provide a suitably atmospheric location for photographing these magnificent birds. The road continues on for 4 miles until Amhuinnsuidhe Castle is reached. A large house in the Scots Baronial style, it is unusual in the fact that the road runs directly past the front door. It now operates a hotel catering for shooting,

Rusty shed on the shoreline with Amhuinnsuidhe Castle in the background (VP1). Fujifilm X–T2, 18–55mm f/2.8–f/4, ISO 200, 1/90s at f/8. Jul.

fishing and events. The castle sits on the shore of Loch Leosay which to the west has a number of interesting bays with rusting sheds and old beached boats sitting amongst irises. The road eventually terminates at the idyllic settlement of Hùisinis, with its pretty white beach overlooked by a few crofthouses. »

How to get here

The road B887 to Hùisinis branches off the A859 6 miles north of Tarbert. It is only 13 miles to Hùisinis, however, the road is very windy and it is likely to take around 30 to 40 minutes.

Viewpoint 1 – The road to Hùisinis (Eagle Observatory)

- **Lat/Long**: 57.950739, -6.9029722
- **what3words**: ///helped.closer.lion
- **Grid Ref**: NB100062
- **Postcode**: HS3 3AW

Viewpoint 2 – Hùisinis & Viewpoint 3 – Tràigh Mheilein

- **Lat/Long**: 57.995592, -7.0913806
- **what3words**: ///automatic.pastels.souk
- **Grid Ref**: NA992120
- **Postcode**: HS3 3AY

Map

OS Landranger Map 14 (1:50 000) Tarbert and Loch Seaforth

Top left: *old boat on the shoreline west of Amhuinnsuidhe Castle. Fujifilm X–T2, 18–55mm f/2.8–f/4, ISO 200, 1/80s at f/8. Jul.* **Top right**: *north or south? Fujifilm X–T2, 18–55mm f/2.8–f/4, ISO 200, 1/130s at f/9. Jul.* **Above**: *a seat on the high point of the road to Huisnis. Fujifilm X–T2, 18–55mm f/2.8–f/4, ISO 200, 1/110s at f/8. Jul.*

Classic cars at Ardhasaig Fujifilm X–T2, 18–55mm f/2.8–f/4, ISO 200, 1/240s at f/11. Sep

7 NORTH HARRIS

The beach at Huisnis (VP2). Fujifilm X–T2, 18–55mm f/2.8–f/4, ISO 200, 1/170s at f/9. Jul.

Viewpoint 2 – Hùisinis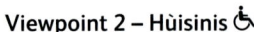

There is a car park above the beach at Hùisinis with excellent facilities for campervans, making it an ideal spot to stay and explore the area. The beach is accessed directly off the road and provides a fine view south to the hills of southern Harris and the hidden beaches on the west side of Taransay. The beach is pleasant enough, but perhaps lacks the photographic appeal of other beaches in Harris. The rocky outcrops at the eastern and western ends provide a useful foil to the white sands.

Viewpoint 3 – Tràigh Mheilein

There are a few beaches in Harris that can lay claim to the title of 'most pretty', however, Tràigh Mheilein must be in with a shout. Perhaps part of its charm is that fact that it is the least easily accessed, at the end of a long road and a steep walk. Even by Hebridean standards it is considered to

Looking north from the machair at Huisnis (VP2). Fujifilm X–T2, 18–55mm f/2.8–f/4, ISO 200, 1/100s at f/9. Jul.

be a quiet beach and it is rare to see anyone else especially outside of peak season. It is in a particular attractive setting, with its white sandy shore lapped by the calm waters of the Kyles of Scarp, and enclosed to the east by rocky hillsides. On the horizon, roughly 5 miles away are the hills of Lewis near Mealasta. They appear tantalisingly close, however, to get there by road would require a 75mile journey! To the west is the now uninhabited isle of Scarp with a collection of isolated buildings now either decaying to ruin or occasionally used as a remote holiday home. Strangely, Scarp was the site of an unsuccessful

Accessibility

Many of the attractions along the road are accessed directly from the road, with the Eagle Observatory a 2km walk on a good path. The beach at Hùisinis is via a short flight of steps. Tràigh Mheilein requires a longer walk up a steep path which is exposed in places with large drops on the seaward side.

Best time of year/day

Hùisinis beach faces south and works well at sunset, at sunrise it is often in shadow due to the hills to the east. Tràigh Mheilein looks like an obvious sunset destination, however, the walk back via the exposed path may be tricky as darkness falls. It may be best to save

this beach for the golden hour at sunset and walk back to Hùisinis to catch the sunset. It equally works well in bright sun, with the aquamarine tones of the water between it and Scarp looking particularly appealing. The road out to Hùisinis is worth traveling at anytime.

Opposite: looking over the Kyles of Scarp to Tràigh Mheilein, Fujifilm X–T2, 18–55mm f/2.8–f/4, ISO 200, 1/60s at f/9. Jul.

7 NORTH HARRIS

The Isle of Scarp. Fujifilm X–T2, 18–55mm f/2.8–f/4, ISO 200, 1/105s at f/8. Jul.

experiment to deliver mail by rocket between the island and Harris and the story features in two films. To reach Tràigh Mheilein head along the road above Hùisinis beach and take the track on the right through the machair. This eventually leads to the slipway on the northern side. Turn right along the shore and aim for the wall at the western end of the shore, a gate gives access onto a path which climbs up steeply to a high point, giving a fantastic view over Tràigh Mheilein and Scarp. The path descends to the southern end of Tràigh Mheilein past some interesting large boulders. There are plenty of compositions to be made on the beach in many directions, the dunes provide plenty of foreground interest. Towards the centre of the beach the views to the east open up towards Loch na Cleabhaig with a pretty little house on its shore which sits in splendid isolation below the hills. At the northern end of the beach, the undulations of the former lazy beds are particularly pronounced in low sun.

Right top: the wild lands to the east of Tràigh Mheilein. Fujifilm X–T2, 18–55mm f/2.8–f/4, ISO 200, 1/105s at f/10. Jul.

The Kyles of Scarp, Fujifilm X–T2, 18–55mm f/2.8–f/4, ISO 200, 1/80s at f/9. Jul.

Tràigh Mheilein and the barren hills of Lewis. Fujifilm X–T2, 18–55mm f/2.8–f/4, ISO 200, 1/105s at f/11. Jul.

8 SCALPAY

The island of Scalpay lies off the eastern coast of Harris connected by the graceful Scalpay bridge which was constructed in 1997. It's a busy wee island and has a population of over 300 with clusters of houses tucked into folds of the land and around the small bays. Fishing was the main industry of the island and today there are still a number of boats setting out to sea from the harbour. The main settlement has a shop and a great restaurant and the harbourside is also worth exploring for all manner of interesting fishing related paraphernalia. The main photographic attraction on the island is the Eilean Glas lighthouse and it's wonderful situation looking out across to Skye.

What to shoot and viewpoints

Viewpoint 1 – Eilean Glas Lighthouse

If you have traveled across the Minch from Uig, you may have seen the Eilean Glas lighthouse on the horizon. With its distinctive red and white bands it is visible from a long distance and is a landmark on the coast. To reach the lighthouse by foot, take the minor road which runs south from the centre of the village. This passes alongside lovely bays, reminiscent of the Golden Road on Harris. After 10 minutes there is a parking area on the left signposted Outend Car Park. From here, head further along the road before taking the path on the left to the lighthouse. This good quality path heads across boggy land, past the wind turbine and after 20 minutes deposits you at the cliffs above Eilean Glas Lighthouse.

The lighthouse makes a fine subject against the backdrop of The Minch with the Shiant Isles and Skye visible on a clear day. From the southern end of the cliffs it is possible to frame the lighthouse against the Shiant Isles. It's worth also walking round the bay to the lighthouse itself and exploring the various outbuildings, some of which are in a various state of disrepair but make a fascinating subjects. The rocks to the south of the lighthouse make a good foreground to the view along the coast as well as providing a good location to see whales and dolphins in the summer months.

How to get here

From Tarbert on Harris, take the minor road east which is signposted to Scalpay. Head over the Scalpay Bridge and follow the road past the shop. There is a parking area on the left hand side of the road signposted Outend Car Park.

Parking

- Lat/Long: 57.859380 , -6.667424
- what3words: ////darker.dustbin.perfumed
- Grid Ref: NG232351
- Postcode: HS4 3YG is 0.762 km from NG232951

Map: OS Landranger Map 14 (1:50 000) Tarbert and Loch Seaforth

Accessibility

The track to the lighthouse is reasonably flat but can be boggy, however it shouldn't post any problems for fit walkers.

Best time of year/day

The lighthouse is a good location to visit on a day of clear visibility where the views across the Minch can be best appreciated. The bright red of the lighthouse looks fantastic in the golden hour at sunset.

Above: *Eilean Glas lighthouse and Skye on the horizon. Fujifilm X–T1, 18–55mm f/2.8–f/4, ISO 200, 1/140s at f/9. Jan.*

Opposite: *Eilean Glas lighthouse. Fujifilm X–T1, 18–55mm f/2.8–f/4, ISO 200, 1/140s at f/9. Jan.*

8 SCALPAY

Top: rainbow over Harris. Fujifilm X–T2, 55–200mm f/3.5–f/4.8, ISO 200, 1/210 at f/9. Oct. **Above left**: ruined croft house on the Harris-side of the Scalpay bridge. Fujifilm X–T2, 10–24mm f/4, ISO 200, 1/1250s at f/6.4. Oct. **Above middle**: fishing boat in the Scalpay harbour. Fujifilm X–T2, 10–24mm f/4, ISO 200, 1/160 s at f/5.6. Oct. **Above right**: Staircase in Eilean Glas lighthouse. Fujifilm X–T1, 18–55mm f/2.8–f/4, ISO 200, 1/80s at f/9. Jan.

Top: sheep in the garden Ceann a Bhàigh. Fujifilm X–T1, 18–55mm f/2.8–f/4, ISO 200, 1/125s at f/9. Jan. **Above left**: houses at Scalpay harbour. Fujifilm X–T2, 55–200mm f/3.5–f/4.8, ISO 200, 1/80 at f/8. Oct. **Above right**: stacked creels near Ceann a Bhàigh. Fujifilm X–T1, 18–55mm f/2.8–f/4, ISO 200, 1/80s at f/9. Jan.

Low tide at Tràigh Ear. Fujifilm X–T2, 18–55mm f/2.8–f/4, ISO 200, 1/450s at f/10. Mar.

OUTER HEBRIDES SOUTH

Cnoc Bhurigh from the south of Berneray. Fujifilm X-T2, 18–55mm f/2.8–f/4, ISO 200, 1/480s at f/8. Aug.

BERNERAY – INTRODUCTION

The name Berneray, like so many others in the Hebrides is of Norse origin and is thought to mean either 'Bjorn's island' or 'Bear Island'. Visiting this small island in the Sound of Harris it is easy to see what would have attracted the viking invaders as they sailed their longships down the Atlantic edge of Scotland. Maybe a fertile low-lying island with a sheltered eastern coast was the perfect place to slow down after a hard life of ocean-going and pillaging. Berneray certainly has a calm and tranquil atmosphere, even the ferry from Harris seems to take a leisurely route to get there, meandering through the skerries and islets of the Sound as if it has all the time in the world.

How to get to Berneray

There is is only one route to Berneray by car and that is via the causeway from North Uist or from Harris by ferry from Leverburgh.

LOCATIONS	
1	Tràigh Iar (West Beach) ... **188**
2	East Beach **192**

Maps

- OS Landranger Map 18 (1:50 000) Sound of Harris, North Uist, Taransay and St Kilda

Previous spread: looking north along Berneray's West Beach from the south. Fujifilm X–T2, 18–55mm f/2.8–f/4, ISO 200, 17s at f/8. Aug.

Opposite: light hits the dunes at the northern end of Tràigh Iar. Fujifilm X–T2, 55–200mm f/3.5–f/4.8, ISO 200, 1/550 at f/9. Oct.

Tràigh Iar from the dunes. Fujifilm X–T2, 18–55mm f/2.8–f/4, ISO 200, 1/1000s at f/8. Oct.

BERNERAY	
Scottish Gaelic	Beàrnaraigh na Hearadh.
Area	4 sq. miles (10 sq. km).
Length/breadth	2.5 × 2 miles.
Highest Elevation	Beinn Shleibhe 93m (305ft).
Owned by	Community buyout ongoing.
Population	138
Largest settlement(s)	Borgh
Vehicles allowed	Yes
Car/Bike rental	Berneray Bikes (Kirkibost), Bespoke Bicycle, Bike Hebrides (Stornoway). Car hire: *carhire-hebrides.co.uk*
Public transport	Yes. Bus timetable at *cne-siar.gov.uk*
Day trips from mainland?	No
Internet/mobile phone coverage	Broadband. 3G/4G dependent on carrier. Poor or no reception away from main towns. Public wifi at ferry terminals and at The Nurse's Cottage (Visitor Centre).
Power	Grid
Island website(s)	*isleofberneray.com* • *isle-of-north-uist.co.uk/isle-of-berneray* *visitouterhebrides.co.uk* • *visitscotland.com* • *scotland.org.uk* *undiscoveredscotland.co.uk*
Festivals/Events	Berneray Week (July) • Music on the Isles (August) *visitouterhebrides.co.uk/whats-on and hebevents.com*
Accommodation	Self-catering, B&Bs, John's Bunkhouse. *isleofberneray.com*
Provisions/Eating Out	Berneray Shop and Bistro, Berneray Post Office (Backhill).
Wildlife	Corncrakes and other long grass nesting birds are common in early summer. Otters, red deer, seals, dolphins, harbour porpoise and several species of whales.
Night Sky Bortle Scale	Class 1.

① BERNERAY

What to shoot and viewpoints

Viewpoint 1 – Tràigh Iar (West Beach)
It is a cliche when describing the Hebrides to say that the beaches look Caribbean or Tropical because of their crystal clear turquoise seas and white sand. However, an image of Tràigh Iar was actually used by the Thai tourist authority to promote Kai Bae beach in Thailand. I'm sure Kai Bae beach is lovely, but I bet you won't get it to yourself (or feel a biting wind off the Atlantic). In all seriousness though, Tràigh Iar is a very special beach, over three miles of white sand, backed by towering dunes and with a truly remarkable vista north along the shore which ends on the peak of Ceapabhal on Harris. It is a magical place. There are plenty of opportunities amongst the dunes, with the marram grass providing a lovely pop of texture against the sand and the elevation emphasising the length of the beach. It is also worth visiting Rubha Bhoisnis at the southern end the beach; a peninsula of grey, wave-scoured rock which juts out into the Atlantic. A lovely contrast to the sand, the intricate geology here provides some fantastic lead in lines to the island of Pabbay. »

Cemetery at Sheabie. Fujifilm X–T2, 18–55mm f/2.8–f/4, ISO 200, 1/70s at f/8. Aug.

Next spread: Tràigh Iar sunset (VP1). Fujifilm X–T2, 18–55mm f/2.8–f/4, ISO 200, 1/10s at f/11. Mar.

How to get here
There is is only one route to Berneray by car and that is via the causeway from North Uist. Once on the island the road winds along the eastern shore past the shop and bistro. To reach viewpoint 1, turn left at the signpost which directs you to Borgh and continue on past the red-roofed community centre on a narrow road through grazing land. After a couple of minutes, the road turns sharply left and there is a small parking area at the corner, from here a gate gives access along a track across the fields to the dunes. To reach viewpoint 2, retrace your route back to eastern side of the island and at the junction turn left, following the road north through the village and past the old harbour. After five minutes, the East beach and the hills of Harris come in to view. There is an informal camping area on the machair and parking is possible along the roadside.

Viewpoint 1 – Tràigh Iar (West Beach)

- **Lat/Long:** 57.707109, -7.2140255
- **what3words:** ///vines.reporting.household
- **Grid Ref:** NF895805
- **Postcode:** HS6 5BJ

Viewpoint 2 – East Beach
- **Lat/Long:** 57.726351, -7.1541881
- **what3words:** ///airbrush.crackles.notice
- **Grid Ref:** NF9328242
- **Postcode:** HS6 5BQ

Map
OS Landranger Map 18 (1:50 000) Sound of Harris, North Uist, Taransay and St Kilda.

Accessibility
Both beaches are very close to the parking areas and easily accessed by able bodied walkers, however, there are steep dunes at Tràigh Iar. The approach to Tràigh Iar is across grazing land so be aware of cattle and give them a wide berth, particular if they have calves.

Best time of year/day
Tràigh Iar is west facing and is a fantastic location for sunset at any time of year. The view north up the beach, with the marram grass lit by the western sun is incredible drawing your eye along the beach to the mountains of north Harris on the horizon. The rocky outcrops at the southern end of Tràigh Iar are best at low to mid-tide and work well in overcast conditions.

Opposite top: rain approaching Tràigh Iar (VP1). Fujifilm X–T2, 18–55mm f/2.8–f/4, ISO 200, 1/640s at f/8. Oct. Bottom left: cows grazing on the machair behind the dunes at Tràigh Iar (VP1). Fujifilm X–T2, 18–55mm f/2.8–f/4, ISO 200, 1/3s at f/11. Mar. Bottom right: the rocky shore at the southern end of Tràigh Iar looking to Pabbay. Fujifilm X–T2, 18–55mm f/2.8–f/4, ISO 200, 20s at f/8. Aug.

1 BERNERAY

Top: East beach. Fujifilm X–T2, 18–55mm f/2.8–f/4, ISO 200, 1/600s at f/8. Aug. **Above**: the youth hostel at East beach. Fujifilm X–T2, 18–55mm f/2.8–f/4, ISO 200, 1/640s at f/11. Oct.

Viewpoint 2 – East Beach

The eastern side of Berneray is very different. A rockier, intricate coastline with houses tucked into folds in the land, huddled down in the lee of the hills which provide shelter from the prevailing westerly winds. Otters are often sighted here, particularity on an incoming tide when they feed. There is also a fantastic beach on the east coast. The outlook is much different, feeling very close to Harris and with distant views which open up to the south east across to the Minch to the Isle of Skye. It is an ideal spot for sunrise over the hills of Harris. The flowering machair which edges up to the sand is beautiful in summer and on a still day the beach can feel positively Tropical or Caribbean.

A ruin behind the youth hostel, Fujifilm X–T2, 18–55mm f/2.8–f/4, ISO 200, 1/10s at f/11. Oct.

Opposite top: looking over to Port Ludaig from the harbour. Fujifilm X–T2, 55–200mm f/3.5–f/4.8, ISO 200, 1/210 at f/5. Oct. **Bottom left**: short-eared owl. Fujifilm X–T2, 55–200mm f/3.5–f/4.8, ISO 200, 1/220 at f/8. Aug. **Bottom right**: East beach at sunset. Fujifilm X–T2, 18–55mm f/2.8–f/4, ISO 200, 1/200s at f/4.5. Aug.

NORTH UIST

NORTH UIST – INTRODUCTION

The island of North Uist is pretty much in the centre of the Outer Hebrides and has examples of all the best elements of this chain of islands. There are wonderful sandy beaches on the west coast and enigmatic isolated peaks rise up from an intricate landscape of bog and lochans which stretch to the east, blending with the sea. It is only with the benefit of elevation that you begin to gain an understanding of the complexities of the landscape.

North Uist sits between the islands of Berneray (where the ferry to Harris arrives and departs) and the island of Benbecula, connected via a causeway which briefly lands on the island of Grimsay. The island is connected to the mainland by the Caledonian MacBrayne service to Uig on Skye which arrives at the main settlement of Lochmaddy. In Lochmaddy there are hotels, a bank, the tourist information and Taigh Chearsabhagh Museum and Arts Centre which has some fantastic exhibitions and an excellent cafe. Also worth a visit is the Hut of Shadows, a stone-built, turf-roofed building which functions as a camera obscura. It is a 10 minute walk north from Lochmaddy towards Sponish, where a suspension bridge crosses a small channel to a headland; the hut is at the eastern end.

There are many interesting historical sites on North Uist which provide photographic opportunities. The chambered cairn at Langass and its ancient stone circle situated as if designed to provide an ideal foreground to the sharks-fin peak of Eabhal in the distance. There is also Trinity Temple at Carnish, with its weathered gravestones and ruined structure rising from the flag irises.

The beaches of North Uist are fantastic, with a real variety on show. There are long white strands which draw the eye north towards the hills of Harris. Or the shallow estuary of Vallay where the tides shift quickly with channels spreading across the sand, and leading the eye across to the ruined structures on the abandoned isle.

For birdwatchers the RSPB reserve at Balranald is a must visit, and on a very clear day you might get to see the archipelago of St Kilda, way out in the Atlantic to the west.

How to get to North Uist

The North Uist ferry runs from Uig on Skye, landing at Lochmaddy. The journey takes 1 hour 45 minutes. You can also get a ferry from Leverburgh on Harris to Berneray, and drive south.

Tràigh Iar from the dunes northwest of Middlequarter. Fujifilm X–T2, 18–55mm f/2.8–f/4, ISO 200, 1/750s at f/8. Oct.

NORTH UIST	
Scottish Gaelic	Uibhist a Tuath.
Area	117 sq. miles (303 sq. km).
Length/breadth	17 × 13 miles.
Highest Elevation	Eaval 347m (1,138ft).
Owned by	Fergus Leveson-Gower, 6th Earl Granville and the North Uist Trust.
Population	1,619
Largest settlement(s)	Lochmaddy
Vehicles allowed	Yes
Car/Bike rental	Bike Uist, Uist Bike Hire, Lasgair Bike Hire, Barra Bike Hire or in Stornoway. Car hire: *carhire-hebrides.co.uk*
Public transport	Yes. Bus timetable at *cne-siar.gov.uk*
Day trips from mainland?	No
Internet/mobile phone coverage	Broadband. 3G/4G dependent on carrier. Poor or no reception away from main towns.
Power	Grid and Wind.
Island website(s)	*www.isle-of-north-uist.co.uk* • *visitouterhebrides.co.uk* • *visitscotland.com* *scotland.org.uk* • *undiscoveredscotland.co.uk*
Festivals/Events	Guided walks at RSPB at Balranald Reserve • St Kilda Challenge (June) *thestkildachallenge.co.uk*. More at *visitouterhebrides.co.uk/whats-on* and *hebevents.com*
Accommodation	Camping, hostels and self-catering at *www.isle-of-north-uist.co.uk/accommodation*
Provisions/Eating Out	There is a shop, phone, bank, hotels and medical facilities; you can buy petrol and diesel in Lochmaddy. On the west coast is the Bayhead shop, fuel and bistro.
Wildlife	Corncrakes at RSBP Nature Reserve at Balranald. Otters, red deer, seals, dolphins, harbour porpoise and several species of whales.
Night Sky Bortle Scale	Class 1.

LOCATIONS

1 The Northern Coast **200**
2 The Atlantic Edge **206**

Maps

- OS Landranger Map 18 (1:50 000) Sound of Harris, North Uist, Taransay and St Kilda

Previous spread: looking west at dawn from Tràigh Hòrnais. Fujifilm X–T2, 18–55mm f/2.8–f/4, ISO 200, 2.5s at f/8. Feb.

Top left: lichen-covered slates on an old house at Balranald. Fujifilm X–T2, 55–200mm f/3.5–f/4.8, ISO 200, 1/2000s at f/5. Oct.
Top right: traditional roofing on a blackhouse. Fujifilm X–T2, 55–200mm f/3.5–f/4.8, ISO 200, 1/3000s at f/4. Oct. **Above left**: sheep feeding on the hillside, Fujifilm X–T2, 55–200mm f/3.5–f/4.8, ISO 200, 1/170s at f/4.7. Mar. **Above right**: geese fly over the ruins at Griminish. Fujifilm X–T2, 55–200mm f/3.5–f/4.8, ISO 200, 1/210s at f/8. Oct.

Top: the Aurora Borealis at Clachan Shannda. Fujifilm X–T2, 14mm f/2.8, ISO 1000, 30s at f/2.8. Mar. **Above left top**: sheep at Port nan Long. Fujifilm X–T2, 18–55mm f/2.8–f/4, ISO 200, 1/400s at f/8. Aug. **Above left bottom**: thatched roof and chimney. Fujifilm X–T2, 18–55mm f/2.8–f/4, ISO 200, 1/60s at f/8. Feb. **Above right**: house at the head of Loch nan Geireann, Fujifilm X–T2, 18–55mm f/2.8–f/4, ISO 200, 1/200s at f/8. Aug.

1 NORTHERN COASTLINE

The northern coastline of North Uist is like no other place in the Hebrides. Endless sands reach out into the Atlantic, with towering sand dunes, flowering machair and tidal lagoons that all vie for the attention. Islands with mysterious ruins appear on the horizon across turquoise water no more than a meter deep. Distant hills appear on the far moorland horizon. It's an intriguing coastline and one which will have the seascape photographer desperate to explore.

What to shoot and viewpoints

Viewpoint 1 – Tràigh Hòrnais and Tràigh Lingeigh
The two beaches of Tràigh Hòrnais and Tràigh Lingeigh are probably the most popular on North Uist. Easily accessed from the B893 these two beaches embody all the key ingredients of classic Hebridean beaches; rolling waves breaking on white shell sand, steep dunes and colourful machair and generally all to yourself, especially at sunrise or sunset. From the picnic area at the end of the track, Tràigh Lingeigh stretches off into the distance with Pabbay, Berneray and Harris appearing on the horizon. Between the two beaches, a rocky headland juts out into the sea, bearing the brunt of the waves. There are a number of compositions to be had in this area, and it offers a great contrast the delicate sands of Tràigh Hòrnais which gracefully arcs away to the west. »

Looking north over Tràigh Lingeigh from Hòrnais (VP1). Fujifilm X–T2, 18–55mm f/2.8–f/4, ISO 200, 1/4s at f/11. Feb.

How to get here

The beaches of North Uist are easily accessed from the road which loops around the island. Tràigh Hòrnais is accessed via the B893 which branches off the A865 4miles northwest of Lochmaddy. At a modern timber house turn left down a track to the cemetery, where parking is available on the left. From here head down the track which ends at a headland between Tràigh Hòrnais and Tràigh Lingeigh. To access Viewpoint 2 take the small road on the left at Grenitote, following it on past the farmhouse and down to a parking area beside the beach where there is space for a few cars at the picnic area. The walk to Tràigh Iar crosses the ford and heads along the the western side of Tràigh Ear before heading across the machair to the dunes. On ascending the dunes Tràigh Iar is revealed. If you wish to explore the full loop round via Tràigh Udal, follow the coastline north and return via Tràigh Ear – this will take roughly two hours. Good views of Tràigh Bhàlaigh can be had from the road at Malacleit.

Viewpoint 1 – Tràigh Hòrnais and Tràigh Lingeigh

- **Lat/Long:** 57.668779, -7.2432517
- **what3words:** ///cabbages.lost.flap
- **Grid Ref:** NF874764
- **Postcode:** HS6 5AY

Viewpoint 2 – Tràigh Iar, Tràigh Udal and Tràigh Ear

- **Lat/Long:** 57.657594, -7.3351639
- **what3words:** ///grinning.threaded.treating
- **Grid Ref:** NF819756
- **Postcode:** HS6 5BP

Viewpoint 3 – Tràigh Bhàlaigh

- **Lat/Long:** 57.649797, -7.3703333
- **what3words:** ///limo.painters.handyman
- **Grid Ref:** NF797749
- **Postcode:** HS6 5BU

Accessibility
All the beaches are very close to the parking areas and easily accessed by able bodied walkers. The walk to Tràigh Udal is longer and pathless but should not pose any navigational difficulties in clear conditions.

Best time of year/day
All west facing beaches in the Hebrides tend to be good sunset locations, however, Tràigh Hòrnais and Tràigh Lingeigh also work well at sunrise, with the low light picking out the islands of Boreray and Lingeigh offshore. How Tràigh Bhàlaigh appears very much depends on the tide; at low tide the network of channels criss-crossing the sand can be interesting in the golden hour and at high tide when combined with bright sun the shallow water turns a fantastic shade of blue.

Looking west from the snow dusted dunes at Tràigh Hòrnais (VP1). Fujifilm X–T2, 18–55mm f/2.8–f/4, ISO 200, 0.8s at f/11. Feb.

Sunrise on a wave at Tràigh Hòrnais. Fujifilm X–T2, 18–55mm f/2.8–f/4, ISO 200, 1/15s at f/11. Feb.

Looking north along Tràigh Hòrnais (VP1). Fujifilm X–T2, 18–55mm f/2.8–f/4, ISO 200, 0.5s at f/11. Feb.

1 NORTHERN COASTLINE

A skim of water over Tràigh Ear (VP2), Fujifilm X–T2, 18–55mm f/2.8–f/4, ISO 200, 1/800s at f/10. Feb.

Viewpoint 2 – Tràigh Iar, Tràigh Udal and Tràigh Ear

These three beaches have quite differing characters. Tràigh Iar is a long stretch of of unbroken sand backed by dunes and machair typical of North Uist. Tràigh Udal is a smaller beach and feels slightly more enclosed with hillocks to the north providing a great outlook to the south. The Udal peninsula has been settled since the neolithic period over 8000 years ago with the fertile landscape as ideal for farming then as it is now. On the eastern side is Tràigh Ear, a wide flat beach with views to the hills of Crògearraidh Mòr and Crògearraidh Beag which are often reflected in tidal pools or a shallow skim of water above the sand. All the beaches can be visited in a 2/3 hour walk. »

Looking to Crògearaidh Mòr from Tràigh Ear, Fujifilm X–T2, 18–55mm f/2.8–f/4, ISO 200, 1/500s at f/10. Feb.

Opposite top: *rain approaching the dunes at Tràigh Udal, Fujifilm X–T2, 18–55mm f/2.8–f/4, ISO 200, 1/480s at f/8. Feb.* **Bottom**: *Tràigh Udal from the dunes (VP2), Fujifilm X–T2, 18–55mm f/2.8–f/4, ISO 200, 1/350s at f/11. Feb.*

1 NORTHERN COASTLINE

Top left: *Restored blackhouse near Malacleit. Fujifilm X–T2, 55–200mm f/3.5–f/4.8, ISO 200, 1/1400s at f/4. Oct.*

A glimpse of the ruins on Vallay from Tràigh Iar. Fujifilm X–T2, 18–55mm f/2.8–f/4, ISO 200, 1/1000s at f/8. Oct.

Big sky above the island of Vallay (VP3). Fujifilm X–T2, 18–55mm f/2.8–f/4, ISO 200, 1/320s at f/11. Feb.

Viewpoint 3 – Tràigh Bhàlaigh

The island of Bhàlaigh/Vallay, shelters a 3km wide tidal estuary and has been unoccupied since the 1940s after tragic death of the last occupant who died crossing the strand. It is possible to walk across at low tide to the island and visit the abandoned buildings, however, the view from the southern shoreline may be enough to satisfy the photographer. At low tide sinuous channels of brackish water wind across the sand, picking up the light and creating elegant patterns and at high tide the shades of blue in the bay are a sight to behold. There is also good scope here for photographing the wading birds and flocks of oystercatchers.

2 THE ATLANTIC EDGE

The west coast of North Uist offers more incredible beaches but also a number of other varied attractions to whet the appetite of the landscape photographer. These viewpoints provide the chance to view the Monach Isles and also the chance to see St Kilda, 40 miles out to sea on the far western horizon. For bird photographers, the RSPB reserve at Balranald offers a chance to encounter a range of birdlife with a couple of great beaches thrown in for good measure. There are also historic sites including Trinity Temple, a neolithic burial chamber and a 400 year old stone circle.

What to shoot and viewpoints

Viewpoint 1 – Scolpaigh Tower
Built in the 1830s by the factor of North Uist, Dr Alexander Macleod, Scolpaigh Tower is an intriguing 8-sided folly on a small islet within Loch Scoplapigh. It was constructed on the site of an Iron Age broch and its construction provided employment for local people suffering from famine. Now home to nesting birds, the tower provides a strong element in the landscape, and makes an ideal silhouette against a sunset sky. It also forms a good mid-ground in the wider view from the road which takes in the loch and the islands of Haskeir on the horizon. »

Blues Brother scarecrow in the fields at Balranald (VP4). Fujifilm X–T2, 18–55mm f/2.8–f/4, ISO 200, 1/800s at f/7.1. Oct.

*Opposite top: Scolpaigh Tower from the roadside (VP1). Fujifilm X–T2, 55–200mm f/3.5–f/4.8, ISO 200, 1/120s at f/8. Oct. **Bottom**: looking across Tràigh Stir from the west (VP2), Fujifilm X–T2, 18–55mm f/2.8–f/4, ISO 200, 1/500s at f/8. Oct.*

How to get here

All the viewpoints are accessed from the A865, directions here are given following the loop road in an anti-clockwise direction from Malacleit. To visit Scolpaigh Tower head west for 5miles on the A865. There are a small number of car parking spaces at the top of the access track which leads down to the tower. It is possible to cross over a causeway to the island on occasions when the water level is particularly low. Tràigh Stir is accessed via a rather bumpy track which branches off the A865 at the turn-off for Hosta, signposted as a picnic area. The track ends behind the dunes, and a short walk over these leads to the beach. The St Kilda View is signposted from the A865 and climbs up the west side of Clettraval for 1.5miles. Balranald has visitor centre with toilet facilities. Head south on the A865 for 1 mile before turning right at the signpost for the RSPB Reserve. After a mile the road forks, take the left side and the parking area is next to the white crofthouse. From here a signposted path can be followed to Tràigh Iar. To access Barpa Langais and Poball Fhinn turn left at Clachan-a-Luib and head along the A867. Take the road on the right to Langass Lodge and park in the small car park. Head through the gate at the end of the road and follow the track which ascends the hillside to the stones. To reach Barpa Langais, return to the A867, turn right and there is a small car park on the right. Trinity Temple is 2.3miles south of Clachan-a-Luib, there is a parking area just off the A865 at Carinish. Form the car park, follow the track past the church and through the gate, the church is reached across a grassy path.

Viewpoint 1 – Scolpaigh Tower

- **Lat/Long**:   57.645004, -7.4764400
- **what3words**: ///exact.flying.niece
- **Grid Ref**:   NF733748
- **Postcode**:   HS6 5DH

2 THE ATLANTIC EDGE

The northeast end of Tràigh Stir (VP2). Fujifilm X–T2, 10–24mm f/4, ISO 200, 1/50s at f/8. Oct.

Viewpoint 2 – Tràigh Stir
Of all the beaches of North Uist, this might just be the most attractive. Roughly north west facing with a glorious sweep of golden sands it is the archetypical Hebridean beach. There are great views to be had from above the beach within the dunes and the rocks at the eastern end offer further intrigue with scope here for macro studies of the striped Lewisian gneiss. It is also possible to scramble around the coast to the equally lovely Tràigh Bheirleal.

Viewpoint 3 – St Kilda view
You might be lucky enough see St Kilda from some of the beaches on the west coast of North Uist, however, the distant archipelago is more easily seen with the aid of elevation. Fortunately, there is a military road which climbs up the side of South Clettraval, serving the radar station of RAF Benbecula. As you ascend the hill, prior to the military

Viewpoint 2 – Tràigh Stir

- **Lat/Long**: 57.626697, -7.4989806
- **what3words**: ///mild.congested.shoulders
- **Grid Ref**: NF718729
- **Postcode**: HS6 5DG

Viewpoint 3 – St Kilda view

- **Lat/Long**: 57.615797, -7.4501917
- **what3words**: ///youngest.duties.nicknames
- **Grid Ref**: NF746715
- **Postcode**: HS6 5DF

Above: *rainstorm approaching the Monach Isles Lighthouse. Fujifilm X–T2, 55–200mm f/3.5–f/4.8, ISO 200, 1/550s at f/8. Mar.*
Far left: *a sheep on the top of South Clettraval (VP3). Fujifilm X–T2, 55–200mm f/3.5–f/4.8, ISO 200, 1/300s at f/4.8. Oct.*
Left: *a golden eagle circles overhead on South Clettraval (VP3). Fujifilm X–T2, 55–200mm f/3.5–f/4.8, ISO 200, 1/420s at f/4.8. Oct.*

Opposite: *a distant St Kilda on the horizon (VP3). Fujifilm X–T2, 55–200mm f/3.5–f/4.8, ISO 200, 1/450s at f/8. Mar.*

Hirta from South Clettraval. Fujifilm X–T2, 55–200mm f/3.5–f/4.8, ISO 200, 1/1250s at f/8. Oct.

Boreray from South Clettraval. Fujifilm X–T2, 55–200mm f/3.5–f/4.8, ISO 200, 1/1250s at f/8. Oct.

THE ATLANTIC EDGE

Ruined house at Balranald. Fujifilm X–T2, 18–55mm f/2.8–f/4, ISO 200, 1/800s at f/7.1. Oct.

buildings is a small walled area next to a parking area. From here there is a fantastic open aspect across the landscape from the north west to the south with far reaching views which (on a clear day) take in St Kilda, the Monach Isles and the hills of South Uist.

Viewpoint 4 – Balranald

Of all the places where you might see a corncrake, the RSPB reserve at Balranald might just be the most likely. Working with local crofters to maintain and improve the habitat, the RSPB at Balranald have made the reserve a key location in the species' long term recovery. Once a common sight throughout the Hebrides, Corncrake numbers plummeted due to changing land uses and differing farming practices. There are also many other birds to be seen at the reserve including dunlin, ringed plover, red shank, and corn bunting as well as wintering ducks and geese. In addition to the ornithological attractions, the loop path from the visitor centre, takes in the croftland, machair and two excellent beaches (with Tràigh Iar being the more attractive) and is well worth visiting even if you aren't a twitcher. »

Viewpoint 4 – Balranald

- **Lat/Long:** 57.605647, -7.5170972
- **what3words:** ///define.huddling.hoped
- **Grid Ref:** NF706707
- **Postcode:** HS6 5DL

Viewpoint 5 – Barpa Langass and Poball Fhinn

- **Lat/Long:** 57.565798, -7.2893385
- **what3words:** ///surfed.kickbacks.nibbles
- **Grid Ref:** NF838651
- **Postcode:** HS6 5HA

Viewpoint 6 – Teampull na Trionaid

- **Lat/Long:** 57.521638, -7.3134659
- **what3words:** ///browsers.dozen.pelt
- **Grid Ref:** NF820603
- **Postcode:** HS6 5EH

Best time of year/day

Scolpaigh Tower makes a fine silhouette at sunset, with the waters of the loch also picking up the sky well however, nearby Tràigh Stir is another great sunset location so it may be a tough choice between the two if you are pushed for time. To make the most of The St Kilda Viewpoint, clear visibility is required. The jagged outlines of islands of Hirta and Boreray (together known as St Kilda) are best photographed at sunset. Balranald RSPB Reserve can be visited at any time. The machair is at its best in June and July and the corncrake makes the long grasses in the fields of Balranald its home from April to September. The stone circle of Poball Fhinn works best in the golden hour towards sunset, where the low rays illuminate both the stones and the wider landscape, it is also better out of the summer months as the bracken can obscure some of the smaller stones.

Opposite top left: *Belted Galloway with Boreray on the horizon (VP4). Fujifilm X–T2, 55–200mm f/3.5–f/4.8, ISO 200, 1/2000s at f/4.8. Oct.* **Top right**: *looking across to Benbecula and South Uist from South Clettraval (VP3). Fujifilm X–T2, 55–200mm f/3.5–f/4.8, ISO 200, 1/200s at f/8. Oct.* **Middle**: *Tràigh Iar at Balranald. Fujifilm X–T2, 18–55mm f/2.8–f/4, ISO 200, 1/8000s at f/7.1. Oct.* **Bottom**: *Poball Fhinn stone circle with Eaval on the horizon (VP5). Fujifilm X–T2, 18–55mm f/2.8–f/4, ISO 200, 1/180s at f/11. Feb.*

Accessibility

All viewpoints are easily accessible. The St Kilda View is essentially roadside. Be careful driving down to Tràigh Stir, the track over the machair is eroded in places and probably not suitable to cars with low suspension. If your car struggles to get over speed bumps, this route isn't for you. The paths at Balranald are flat and the beach is easily accessed. There is a gravel path to Barpa Langais and a narrow, slightly boggy path to Poball Fhinn from Langass Lodge.

2 THE ATLANTIC EDGE

Viewpoint 5 – Barpa Langass and Poball Fhinn

A short detour back inland leads to two of North Uist's most important Neolithic sites; Barpa Langass and Poball Fhinn (Finn's People). The chambered cairn of Barpa Langass is not the most photographically interesting, although it's quite a dramatic sight with a 25m radius of rough stone enclosing a hidden burial chamber. The elevated viewpoint also gives a good overview of the interior landscape of moorland and hills with distant views across the island. Just to the southeast, on the shore of Loch Langais is the stone circle of Poball Fhinn which is thought to be over 4000 years old. The stones are arrayed in a loose oval, popping out of overgrown heather and bracken and forming a great foreground for the view to the east dominated by the hill Eabhal.

Viewpoint 6 – Teampull na Trionaid

There is some ambiguity to the origins of the Trinity Temple with sources claiming it as a nunnery, a monastery or even Scotlands oldest university. The ruin sits up on a small hillock above the Feith na Fala, the Ditch of Blood, the site of a fierce battle between Macleods and Mcdonalds and forms an interesting tumbled down silhouette on the skyline. The curved wall along the southern elevation make a fine study, particularly against the swaying flag iris in spring and summer.

*Top: Poball Fhinn stone circle (VP5). Fujifilm X–T2, 18–55mm f/2.8–f/4, ISO 200, 18s at f/8. Aug. **Middle**: Barpa Langass. Fujifilm X–T2, 18–55mm f/2.8–f/4, ISO 200, 1/1100s at f/8. Feb. **Bottom**: ruin beside Loch Langais. Fujifilm X–T2, 18–55mm f/2.8–f/4, ISO 200, 1/150s at f/8. Feb.*

***Opposite top**: Trinity Temple from the south. Fujifilm X–T2, 18–55mm f/2.8–f/4, ISO 200, 6s at f/8. Aug. **Opposite left**: Trinity Temple on the approach from the east. Fujifilm X–T2, 18–55mm f/2.8–f/4, ISO 200, 1/4s at f/11. Aug.*

The church at Carinish on the way to Trinity Temple. Fujifilm X–T2, 18–55mm f/2.8–f/4, ISO 200, 1/350s at f/8. Aug.

Top row: reeds in a lochan at Griminish. Fujifilm X–T2, 18–55mm f/2.8–f/4, ISO 200, 1/280s at f/8. Oct. **Middle**: thatched roof weighed down with rocks, Fujifilm X–T2, 18–55mm f/2.8–f/4, ISO 200, 1/60s at f/5. Feb. **Right**: rusty shed near Blathaisbhal. Fujifilm X–T2, 18–55mm f/2.8–f/4, ISO 200, 1/1250s at f/8. Aug. **Above left**: rock and roof detail. Fujifilm X–T2, 18–55mm f/2.8–f/4, ISO 250, 1/60s at f/8. Feb. **Above right**: cottage above the beach near Malacleit. Fujifilm X–T2, 55–200mm f/3.5–f/4.8, ISO 800, 1/60s at f/4.8. Mar. **Opposite middle left**: roofless house near Strumore. Fujifilm X–T2, 18–55mm f/2.8–f/4, ISO 200, 1/150s at f/8. Mar. **Middle right**: blackhouse at Clachan Shannda, Fujifilm X–T2, 18–55mm f/2.8–f/4, ISO 200, 1/120s at f/11. Mar. **Bottom**: blackhouse with Vallay on the horizon beyond. Fujifilm X–T2, 18–55mm f/2.8–f/4, ISO 200, 1/900s at f/8. Oct.

BENBECULA

BENBECULA

Benbecula sits in the centre of the long chain of islands often referred to as the Uists which form the edge of the Atlantic seaboard of the Hebrides. It is connected to the north and south by causeways and there is also an airport, with daily flights connecting the island to Glasgow and Stornoway. It is the main administrative centre of the region with supermarkets, schools and sports facilities.

A mainly low-lying island studded with lochans, Benbecula has lots of interest to photograph including wonderful sandy beaches and the hill of Ruabhal which provides a sensational view.

How to get to Benbecula

Drive
You get to Benbecula by driving across the causeway from North Uist or South Uist.

Air
It's an hour flight from Glasgow to Benbecula Airport. Flights also leave Edinburgh and Inverness to the airport. Details at: *loganair.co.uk*

Looking across to South Uist from Creagorry at the southern end of Benbecula. Fujifilm X–T2, 18–55mm f/2.8–f/4, ISO 200, 1/300s at f/8. Mar.

BENBECULA	
Scottish Gaelic	Beinn na Faoghla.
Area	31 sq. mi (80 sq. km).
Length/breadth	7 × 7 miles.
Highest Elevation	Ruabhal, 124m (407ft).
Owned by	Stòras Uibhist a community owned company manages the 93,000 acre South Uist Estate comprising of Eriskay, South Uist and parts of Benbecula.
Population	1,283
Largest settlement(s)	Balivanich (main village), Nunton, Lionacleit & Creagory (hamlets).
Vehicles allowed	Yes
Car/Bike rental	Bike Uist, Uist Bike Hire, Lasgair Bike Hire, Barra Bike Hire or in Stornoway. Car hire: *carhire-hebrides.co.uk*
Public transport	Yes. Bus timetable at *cne-siar.gov.uk*
Day trips from mainland?	No
Internet/mobile phone coverage	Broadband. 3G/4G dependent on carrier. Poor or no reception away from main towns.
Power	Grid
Island website(s)	*www.isle-of-benbecula.co.uk/ • visitouterhebrides.co.uk • visitscotland.com scotland.org.uk • undiscoveredscotland.co.uk*
Festivals/Events	Eilean Dorcha Festival (July) *visitouterhebrides.co.uk/whats-on and hebevents.com*
Accommodation	There are a couple of hotels, several B&Bs, a hostel and a campsite. More at *www.isle-of-benbecula.co.uk/accommodation*
Provisions/Eating Out	Balivanich has a post office, hospital, primary school and several shops and cafes. Eating out includes Old Creagorry Bar, Charlie's Bistro & Stepping Stone Restaurant in Balivanich.
Wildlife	The Uists and Benbecula are noted for their breeding mute swan and greylag geese as well as Whooper swans and white-fronted geese and duck. Otters, red deer, seals, dolphins, harbour porpoise and several species of whales.
Night Sky Bortle Scale	Class 1.

LOCATIONS

1 Ruabhal **222**
2 Culla **226**

Maps

- OS Landranger Map 22 (1:50 000) Benbecula & South Uist

Previous spread: looking across to Eabhal from Ruabhal.
Fujifilm X–T2, 55–200mm f/3.5–f/4.8, ISO 200,
1/240s at f/8. Oct.

1 BENBECULA

What to shoot and viewpoints

Viewpoint 1 – Ruabhal

The landscape of Benbecula is typical of much of the western isles. A landscape of real contrast. If you imagine viewing from it from the air, in the west, there is the Atlantic coast defined by sandy beaches backed by dunes, machair and fertile farmland. As the eye gazes inland to the east, the farmland gives way to a mixture of heathery rocks and boggy moorland studded by thousands of lochans glinting in the sun. On the eastern coast, sea lochs bite deeply into the land, raggedly serrating the coast. It begins to become difficult to ascertain whether this is a landscape of moorland which cradles lochs within it or a seascape punctuated with islands of moorland. This view is not generally seen without the use of a drone, however, walkers can obtain this view from the summit of Ruabhal, located in the centre of Benbecula. At a mere 124m, this wee hill gives a view which far bigger peaks struggle to match. Panning round from the north, there is Harris and North Uist with the great of sharks-fin of Eabhal dominating the view. To the west the lighthouse of Hyskeir and beyond, on a clear day, St Kilda appearing on the horizon. To the south the towering hills of South Uist loom over the landscape. Then to the southeast the islands of Rum, Canna and Skye. You begin to feel that you aren't

Clouds passing over Eabhal. Fujifilm X–T2, 55–200mm f/3.5–f/4.8, ISO 200, 1/340s at f/8. Oct.

on the edge, you are right in the centre the Hebrides. The opportunities are varied here; wide shots of the whole landscape in all directions are possible, but a telephoto lens also opens up the possibility of homing in on smaller elements in the landscape like the patterns of the lochans or the scattered houses, strung out along the sea lochs to the east. »

How to get here

Benbecula is a small island and both viewpoints are easily reached. To access Ruabhal, head south on the A865 and at the Recycling Centre (a large red shed) turn left down a minor road. There is a parking area on the left hand side as the road descends. From here walk east along a good track until reaching a loch on the right. Take the faint path on the left which rises up the hill. The walk up takes roughly 30 minutes. Culla beach is almost due west of Ruabhal, and is only a 10 minute drive away. Return to the recycling centre and at the crossroads head across, continuing down a single track road. Once the B892 is reached, turn right and then take the next road on the left. At the T-junction turn left and there is a small parking and picnic area at the end of the road. From here a path gives access to the beach via the dunes.

Viewpoint 1 – Ruabhal

- **Lat/Long:** 57.458617, -7.3178667
- **what3words:** ///area.lightbulb.nozzle
- **Grid Ref:** NF812534
- **Postcode:** HS7 5LY

Viewpoint 2 – Culla

- **Lat/Long:** 57.463423, -7.4019110
- **what3words:** ///cunning.wriggled.adopt
- **Grid Ref:** NF762543
- **Postcode:** HS7 5LU

Accessibility

The summit of Ruabhal is easily reached by fit walkers in around 20/30 minutes although the route up can be boggy in places. There is a path so route finding should not be difficult. Culla bay is essentially roadside, however, the dunes are steep in places. It is possible to follow the track further to the west to gain access the the beach without climbing the dunes.

Best time of year/day

Both viewpoints work well at sunset and it would almost be possible to combine the two in an evening as they are very close to each other. Ruabhal really needs a clear day where the far-reaching views can be best experienced. On a few very clear days, St Kilda can be seen on the far western horizon.

Jo and Alfie waiting for the light on Ruabhal. Fujifilm X–T2, 18–55mm f/2.8–f/4, ISO 200, 1/480s at f/8. Oct.

Looking over Balivanich from Ruabhal. Fujifilm X–T2, 18–55mm f/2.8–f/4, ISO 200, 1/480s at f/8. Aug.

Top: *a distant view of Neist Point Lighthouse on Skye from Ruabhal. Fujifilm X–T2, 55–200mm f/3.5–f/4.8, ISO 200, 1/320s at f/8. Oct.*

Looking south from Ruabhal over the lochs to South Uist. Fujifilm X–T2, 18–55mm f/2.8–f/4, ISO 200, 1/240s at f/8. Oct.

1. BENBECULA

Looking north west to North Uist from Ruabhal, Fujifilm X–T2, 55–200mm f/3.5–f/4.8, ISO 200, 1/550s at f/8. Oct.

Viewpoint 2 – Culla

Exhibiting the western side of the islands best character is the beach at Culla. A classic Hebridean sandy beach, it has much to offer the seascape photographer. The dunes at the northern end provide a good elevated view of the sweep of sand terminating at a farmhouse with the mountains of South Uist appearing on the distant horizon. The fields behind the beach are home to the corncrake and you may hear their rasping 'crek crek' call, particularly in the evening. They are a shy bird though and you will be very lucky if you see one.

Opposite top: in amongst the dunes at the north of Cula beach, Fujifilm X–T2, 18–55mm f/2.8–f/4, ISO 200, 14s at f/8. Aug.
Bottom: two-tone sand on Cula beach, Fujifilm X–T2, 18–55mm f/2.8–f/4, ISO 200, 10s at f/8. Aug.

Previous spread: the intricate landscape of lochs, sea and land to the south of Ruabhal. Fujifilm X–T2, 18–55mm f/2.8–f/4, ISO 200, 1/300s at f/8. Oct.

Cula beach from the path along the dunes. Fujifilm X–T2, 18–55mm f/2.8–f/4, ISO 200, 4.5s at f/8. Aug.

SOUTH UIST

The long island of South Uist runs from Benbecula in the north to Eriskay in the south. It's an island of extreme contrasts. The west coast has miles and miles of sandy beaches which run in an unbroken chain along the Atlantic shore. Behind these is a band of machair and fertile croft land. The land then changes, rearing up to large, rocky peaks which are patrolled by eagles. Around the feet of these hills are countless lochans. A complicated network, where it is difficult to establish where the land stops and the sea begins.

The main settlement of South Uist is Lochboisdale, the east-facing port town at the southern end of the island, it is here that you will arrive on the island if you have sailed on the Caledonian MacBrayne service from Oban, Mallaig or Uig. At the northern end of the island, South Uist is connected via causeway to Benbecula and at the south another causeway connects it to Eriskay. Lochboisdale is the main settlement and has a hotel, tourist information centre and around the bay at the new marina is the excellent Skydancer Art Café.

The beaches of South Uist are world renowned, and with almost 20 miles of coastline, you are bound to find some solitude. In spring and summer, the machair behind the beaches comes alive with a dazzling display of wildflowers; a truly rare habitat. Inland, a quiet single track road runs out to Loch Sgioport where you are likely to encounter free-roaming ponies. At the large freshwater Loch Druidibeag, managed by the RSPB, watch out for hen harriers and eagles and take a walk to the lochside, where you can photograph the hills of Hecla and Beinn Mhor. At Howmore there are some beautiful old thatched roof cottages which give a tantalising glimpse into the past and a wonderful white church which pops out against the surrounding fields. Fans of Brutalist architecture will be delighted by the imposing church of Our Lady of Sorrows.

How to get to South Uist

Drive
South Uist can be reached by driving south from Benbecula over the causeway.

Ferry
You can get to South Uist by ferry from Mallaig and Oban, which arrives at Lochboisdale. This crossing from Mallaig takes 3 hours 30 minutes. The crossing from Oban takes 5 hours 10 minutes. Vehicle reservations are recommended. Oban-Lochboisdale is a winter service only. Ferries also connect Barra with South Uist.

Air
It's an hour flight from Glasgow to Benbecula or Barra Airport. Flights also leave Edinburgh and Inverness to the airports. Details at: **loganair.co.uk**. You can then drive to South Uist. You can rent a car on Barra, details at: **carhire-hebrides.co.uk**

Previous spread: going fishing on Loch Bi. Fujifilm X–T2, 18–55mm f/2.8–f/4, ISO 200, 1/600s at f/8. Aug.

SOUTH UIST	
Scottish Gaelic	Uibhist a Deas.
Area	124 sq. mi (321 sq. km).
Length/breadth	20 × 7 miles.
Highest Elevation	Beinn Mhòr 620m (2,030 ft).
Owned by	Stòras Uibhist a community owned company manages the 93,000 acre South Uist Estate comprising of Eriskay, South Uist and parts of Benbecula.
Population	1,897
Largest settlement(s)	Lochboisdale (Tourist Office), Daliburgh, Snishvale, Eochar, Polochar.
Vehicles allowed	Yes
Car/Bike rental	Bike Uist, Uist Bike Hire, Lasgair Bike Hire, Barra Bike Hire or in Stornoway. Car hire: *carhire-hebrides.co.uk*
Public transport	Yes. Bus timetable at *cne-siar.gov.uk*
Day trips from mainland?	No
Internet/mobile phone coverage	Broadband. 3G/4G dependent on carrier. Poor or no reception away from main towns.
Power	Grid and Wind.
Island website(s)	*isle-of-south-uist.co.uk* • *visitouterhebrides.co.uk* • *visitscotland.com* *scotland.org.uk* • *undiscoveredscotland.co.uk*
Festivals/Events	Ceolas Summer School (July). More at *visitouterhebrides.co.uk/whats-on* and *hebevents.com*
Accommodation	Orasay Inn & Polochar Inn are hotels, along with self-catering, camping and B&Bs. Listing at *isle-of-south-uist.co.uk/accommodation*
Provisions/Eating Out	Hebridean Jewellery Coffee Shop, Kilbride Cafe, Kildonan Museum and Coffee Shop, Salar Smokehouse, Orasay Inn. Lovats Supermarket – Carnan, South Uist, Co-op Food – Daliburgh.
Wildlife	White tailed eagle (Loch Sgioport/Loch Druidibeg on South Uist), hen harrier and short-eared owl as well as many wading birds, otters, red deer, seals, dolphins, harbour porpoise and several species of whales.
Night Sky Bortle Scale	Class 1.

LOCATIONS
1 The beaches **232**
2 Lochs and mountains **240**

Maps

- OS Landranger Map 31 (1:50 000) Barra & South Uist, Vatersay & Eriskay

1. THE BEACHES

The coast of South Uist is characterised by an almost unbroken sandy shoreline which stretches for the 20 mile length of the Atlantic foreshore. Whilst not as immediately photogenic as some other Hebridean beaches, there is a bleak beauty about these windswept strands. Immediately behind the beaches is the Machair, the name given to what is one of the rarest habitats in Europe. The machair is created by shell sand, blown in from the beaches on the Atlantic wind which then breaks down, creating a fertile calcium rich soil. This natural process, coupled with traditional crofting practices of low intensity rotational farming created the perfect environment for the growth of wild flowers. From May onwards the machair is a patchwork of wild flowers, the colours of which change throughout the summer. It is a beautiful sight and will delight macro photographers and anyone with an interest in wildflowers.

The viewpoints chosen are by no means an exhaustive list of all the beaches on South Uist, but have been picked as they offer a bit more than just a long sandy shoreline.

What to shoot and viewpoints

Viewpoint 1 – Tobha Mor ♿
The village of Tobha Mor (Howmore) has a remarkable number of interesting buildings. There are ruined churches and traditional thatched blackhouses many of which provide scope for interesting compositions. There is a small parking area outside Howmore Church, a fine white-rendered church which pops up in the view from the beach against the dark mountains behind. The beach at Howmore is accessed a short walk from the church where a peaty stream flows out across the white sand. »

How to get here
Howmore is 13 miles north of Lochboisdale on a minor road which branches off the A865. The turn off to Garrynamonie is 13 miles south of Daliburgh just after the church of Our Lady of Sorrows. For the beaches along the south coast proceed south from the church following signs to Eriskay. Parking areas are scarce along the road with no dedicated spaces and combining your trip with a visit to the excellent Kilbride Cafe is probably the best option.

Viewpoint 1 – Tobha Mor

- Lat/Long: 57.302499, -7.3871694
- what3words: ///fashion.cakewalk.enveloped
- Grid Ref: NF756363
- Postcode: HS8 5SH

Viewpoint 2 – Geàrraidh an Mònadh

- Lat/Long: 57.121750, -7.3896622
- what3words: ///depths.dinosaur.tolls
- Grid Ref: NF739163
- Postcode: HS8 5TX

Viewpoint 3 – Cùl-Phort

- Lat/Long: 57.103345, -7.3561841
- what3words: ///duke.stooping.stereos
- Grid Ref: NF758141
- Postcode: HS8 5TT

Accessibility
All viewpoints are close to parking areas and are accessible to walkers within a short distance. The beaches on the west coast are huge and you could walk for miles if you so choose.

Best time of year/day
Undoubtedly the star of the show in South Uist is the machair so if you are planning to photograph it visit between May and September. The colour varies throughout the season but tends to be at its best and most intense in July. The beaches on the west coast are obvious sunset destinations but are also well worth visiting on blustery winter days, especially if you feel your skin could do with exfoliation. The smaller tidal beaches along the south coast work best at mid to low tide, at high tide most of the sand is covered.

Opposite top: the church at Howmore from the fields (VP1). Fujifilm X–T2, 18–55mm f/2.8–f/4, ISO 200, 1/420s at f/8. Aug.
Bottom: Howmore beach. Fujifilm X–T2, 18–55mm f/2.8–f/4, ISO 200, 1/500s at f/8. Aug.

Overleaf: wildflower machair at Howmore. Fujifilm X–T2, 18–55mm f/2.8–f/4, ISO 200, 1/600s at f/8. Aug.

1 THE BEACHES

Top left: *flowering meadows at Howmore (VP1). Fujifilm X–T2, 55–200mm f/3.5–f/4.8, ISO 200, 1/550s at f/8. Aug.* ***Top right***: *traditional blackhouse beside Howmore church. Fujifilm X–T2, 55–200mm f/3.5–f/4.8, ISO 200, 1/250s at f/4.8. Aug.* ***Middle left***: *grasses in the machair. Fujifilm X–T2, 55–200mm f/3.5–f/4.8, ISO 200, 1/250s at f/4.8. Aug.* ***Middle right***: *flowers on Howmore beach. Fujifilm X–T2, 18–55mm f/2.8–f/4, ISO 200, 1/1200s at f/5.6. Aug.* ***Bottom left***: *Howmore beach from the dunes. Fujifilm X–T2, 18–55mm f/2.8–f/4, ISO 200, 1/640s at f/8. Aug.* ***Bottom right***: *clover in the machair. Fujifilm X–T2, 55–200mm f/3.5–f/4.8, ISO 200, 1/350s at f/4.8. Aug.*

Four studies of Our Lady of Sorrows (VP2).

Viewpoint 2 – Geàrraidh an Mònadh

The beach at Garrynamonie is accessed from a small picnic area at the end of manor road which branches off the B888 at the brutalist church of Our Lady of Sorrows. The church itself (like most Brutalist architecture) divides opinion but its striking lines and bold, bluff facades make a fascinating study. The beach itself is backed by wonderful machair and the tidal island of Orasaigh at its northern end helps to provide a termination point to the view. »

1 THE BEACHES

The beach at Cùl-Phort looking over to Eriskay (VP3). Fujifilm X–T2, 18–55mm f/2.8–f/4, ISO 200, 1/75s at f/10. Aug.

Viewpoint 3 – Cùl-Phort

The photographer Paul Strands book Tir a' Mhurain is one of the great photographic studies of the Hebrides. Visiting in 1945 over a period of three months, Strand documented the people and and the landscape of South Uist in an honest, non-romanticised way, publishing his book in 1962. The cover image is an evocative image of the South Uist coast with horses roaming the beach in front of a small crofthouse, perched out on the rocks. That house is still there today. You obviously do not need to slavishly replicate Strands image (indeed you can't as the Eriskay Causeway was not built then and now appears in the view), but there are some lovely opportunities along this stretch of coastline with a mixture of rocky outcrops and a fantastic view across to Eriskay giving it a real contrast to the other beaches on South Uist.

An old bus in a field at Cùl-Phort. Fujifilm X–T2, 18–55mm f/2.8–f/4, ISO 200, 1/200s at f/8. Aug.

Looking north to Orasaigh from the dunes along the beach at Garrynamonie (VP2). Fujifilm X–T1, 18–55mm f/2.8–f/4, ISO 200, 1/125s at f/8. Dec.

2 LOCHS AND MOUNTAINS

The eastern side of South Uist has a completely different character to that of the west. Gone are the beaches and machair, replaced by a windswept landscape of loch, mountain and bog. Sea lochs reach in from the east, weaving their way deep inland forming sheltered bays. Accessed from the west, narrow roads running eastwards pass isolated houses tucked into nooks in the land. Mountains dominate the landscape, difficult to access and remote to all but the most determined hill walkers. The east coast itself is totally roadless and almost pathless, a remote and wild landscape facing towards Skye.

What to shoot and viewpoints

Viewpoint 1 – Loch Bi

Loch Bi is the largest loch in South Uist and is actually connected to the sea at both sides, northwest at Clachan and via Loch Sheilavaig to the south east, effectively carving South Uist into two islands. It is crossed by the A865 which follows the line of the causeway built in the 18th century. The loch is a popular fishing location and from the parking area there are usually a couple of rowing boats tied up in the shallows. On a still day these are reflected in the loch and make a perfect foreground for the view across the water to the mountains of Hecla and Beinn Mhor.

Viewpoint 2 – RSPB Loch Druidibeag and Loch Sgioport

Loch Druidibeag is an extensive freshwater loch located to the north of the highest peaks in South Uist; Hecla and Beinn Mhor. The area is managed as a Nature Reserve by the RSPB and is home to Hen Harriers and White Tailed eagles. There is a new track which runs west from the parking area, however, there are better views of the loch to the southeast. A good pair of waterproof boots will see you through the boggy ground and down to the edge of the loch amongst a carpet of heather and fragrant bog myrtle. There are many

Opposite: rowing boat in Loch Bi (VP1). Fujifilm X–T2, 18–55mm f/2.8–f/4, ISO 200, 120s at f/8. Aug.

How to get here

South Uist is accessed by ferry from Oban which sails to Lochboisdale in the south and is reached from the north by the causeway from Benbecula. These viewpoints are both accessed off the A865. From the north, on approach to Loch Bi there is parking area on the right hand side of the road. Cross the road and access the loch shore via the gate. Loch Druidibeag is reached via a minor road which branches off the A865 to the left a further 2.4miles to the south of Loch Bi. The road weaves its way along the loch side before the obvious parking area is reached on the right hand side. Loch Sgioport is a further 3 miles along the road. To get to the pier, park at the end of the paved road and walk the last few hundred metres (the road is not suitable for vehicles except 4x4s).

Viewpoint 1 – Loch Bi

- **Lat/Long**: 57.363283, -7.3547750
- **what3words**: ///swing.nips.orbit
- **Grid Ref**: NF781429
- **Postcode**: HS8 5RP

Viewpoint 2 – Loch Druidibeag

- **Lat/Long**: 57.321209, -7.3353861
- **what3words**: ///divided.flats.handsets
- **Grid Ref**: NF789382
- **Postcode**: HS8 5RR

Viewpoint 3 – Loch Sgioport

- **Lat/Long**: 57.327003, -7.2742444
- **what3words**: ///lied.masses.value
- **Grid Ref**: NF826385
- **Postcode**: HS8 5NS

Accessibility

Generally easily accessed with a short walk required across boggy, heathery terrain to each the shores of Loch Druidibeag. The shore of Loch Bi can be boggy and slippery.

Best time of year/day

Both viewpoints are south facing so are best avoided in the middle of the day. The mountains are seen at their best in the golden hour prior to sunset when the low sun picks up their rocky slopes, heightening the drama. The heather comes into bloom in late summer and can add interest to foregrounds, particularly at Loch Druidibeag. If your visit coincides with a rare winter snowfall, the mountains can look especially dramatic from either viewpoint.

Loch Druidibeag (VP2). Fujifilm X–T2, 18–55mm f/2.8–f/4, ISO 200, 1/25s at f/10. Aug.

Sheep on an island in Loch Bi. Fujifilm X–T2, 18–55mm f/2.8–f/4, ISO 200, 1/900s at f/8. Aug.

SOUTH UIST – LOCHS AND MOUNTAINS

2 LOCHS AND MOUNTAINS

Above: one of the scattered islands in Loch Druidibeag (VP2). Fujifilm X–T2, 18–55mm f/2.8–f/4, ISO 200, 60s at f/11. Aug.
Top: looking over Loch Bi to the mountains of South Uist (VP1). Fujifilm X–T2, 18–55mm f/2.8–f/4, ISO 200, 1/120s at f/8. Aug.

opportunities for compositions along the lochshore, with the stunted trees on the islands providing a good mid-ground. At the far end of the road is lonely Loch Sgioport with its tumbledown pier giving melancholy feel to the landscape. This area is home to a band of free-roaming ponies who have now become wise to visitors and expect a toll for having their photo taken. This is to be paid in carrots.

Middle right: Heather in bloom along the shore of Loch Druidibeag. Fujifilm X–T2, 18–55mm f/2.8–f/4, ISO 200, 1/320s at f/5.6. Aug. **Right**: Bog Myrtle and Heather. Fujifilm X–T2, 18–55mm f/2.8–f/4, ISO 200, 1/150s at f/8. Aug.

Above: the remnants of the pier at Lochskipport (VP2). Fujifilm X–T2, 18–55mm f/2.8–f/4, ISO 200, 1/200s at f/10. Oct **Top**: the old postman's house near Lochskipport (VP2). Fujifilm X–T2, 55–200mm f/3.5–f/4.8, ISO 200, 1/550s at f/8. Oct.

One of the free-roaming ponies. Fujifilm X–T2, 18–55mm f/2.8–f/4, ISO 200, 1/420s at f/6.4. Oct.

ERISKAY

ERISKAY – INTRODUCTION

The Isle of Eriskay is only a small island but is world famous for many reasons aside from its beautiful landscape of beaches, rocky hills and sheltered coves.

It is the home of the Eriskay Pony, a critically endangered species, the last remnants of the wild ponies which were once found throughout the Western Isles. Prior to the building of the causeway Eriskay was a hard place to reach and unlike many other places in the Hebrides, alternative species were not introduced. This has resulted in a pure stock of these hardy, friendly and beautiful animals. The Eriskay Jersey, a traditional fisherman's jumper woven without seams for warmth at sea is from the island. Usually produced in blue or cream, the jersey often incorporated intricate patterns distinctive to each family. However, Eriskay is probably most famous for the events surrounding the sinking of the SS Politician, a story celebrated in the book and subsequent film Whisky Galore. On 5th February 1941 the ship ran aground off the coast of Eriskay and amongst its cargo of cotton, bicycles, Jamaican dollars, clothes and biscuits were 22,000 cases of Whisky; a scarce commodity on a Hebridean island during the war. Many of these cases were looted by the locals who buried them in caches across the island in order to thwart the recovery efforts of the Customs and Excise men. One man even hid 46 cases in a cave on neighbouring Barra! Not all of the 264,000 bottles were recovered, but you would imagine there was enough whisky to keep the local ceilidhs going for a good few years!

The only pub on Eriskay (appropriately named Am Politician) has a few of the bottles behind the bar.

How to get to Eriskay

Drive
Drive across the causeway from South Uist to Eriskay.

Ferry
You can get to Eriskay on the ferry from Ardmhor, Barra. The journey takes 40 minutes. Vehicle reservations are recommended.

Hebridean sheep at Haun. Fujifilm X–T1, 55–200mm f/3.5–f/4.8, ISO 200, 1/550s at f/4.5. Dec.

Sheep posing in front of the isle of Lingeigh. Fujifilm X–T2, 18–55mm f/2.8–f/4, ISO 200, 1/1400s at f/6.4. Mar.

ERISKAY	
Scottish Gaelic	Èirisgeigh.
Area	2.75 sq. mi (7 sq. km).
Length/breadth	2.5 × 1.5 miles.
Highest Elevation	Beinn Sgrithean 185.6m (609ft).
Owned by	Stòras Uibhist a community owned company manages the 93,000 acre South Uist Estate comprising of Eriskay, South Uist and parts of Benbecula.
Population	143
Largest settlement(s)	Balla
Vehicles allowed	Yes
Car/Bike rental	Bike Uist, Uist Bike Hire, Lasgair Bike Hire, Barra Bike Hire or in Stornoway. Car hire: *carhire-hebrides.co.uk*
Public transport	Yes. Bus timetable at *cne-siar.gov.uk*
Day trips from mainland?	No
Internet/mobile phone coverage	Broadband. 3G/4G dependent on carrier. Poor or no reception away from main towns.
Power	Grid and Wind.
Island website(s)	*isle-of-south-uist.co.uk/isle-of-eriskay* • *outaboutscotland.com/isle-of-eriskay* *visitouterhebrides.co.uk* • *visitscotland.com* • *scotland.org.uk* *undiscoveredscotland.co.uk*
Festivals/Events	*visitouterhebrides.co.uk/whats-on* and *hebevents.com*
Accommodation	B&Bs, self-catering.
Provisions/Eating Out	Eriskay Community Shop and the Politician pub.
Wildlife	Eriskay Ponies (Each Beag nan Eilean), seals, dolphins, harbour porpoise and several species of whales. Bonnie Prince Charlie's Flower.
Night Sky Bortle Scale	Class 1.

LOCATIONS

1. Prince Charlies Beach **248**
2. The village **250**

Maps

- OS Landranger Map 31 (1:50 000) Barra & South Uist, Vatersay & Eriskay

Previous spread: Coilleag a' Phrionnsa. Fujifilm X–T2, 18–55mm f/2.8–f/4, ISO 200, 60s at f/8. Aug.

1 ERISKAY

What to shoot and viewpoints

Viewpoint 1 – Prince Charlies Beach

Another of Eriskay's claims to fame is that it is the site where Bonnie Prince Charlie landed in 1745 at the start of his ill-fated Jacobite Rebellion which sought to regain the throne of Britain for his father. It ended with defeat on Culloden Moor in 1746 and brought about the beginning of the end for much of the traditional highland clan system. However, he gives his name to this wonderful stretch of beach; Coilleag a' Phrionnsa (The Prince's Cockle Strand) a simply delightful white sand bay with an outlook to the islands of Luday, South Uist and Barra. There are some great opportunities along the beach, however, the most interesting point is at the southern end where the white sand gives way to black rocks. This gives a lovely contrast which works particulate well in long exposure shots, rendering the shallow water above the sand a milky turquoise colour. »

How to get here

From Lochboisdale in South Uist head north west out of the village on the A865 until you reach the village of Daliburgh. On passing a church on the left take the B888, after 10 minutes turn left at the bus stop. The road winds its way along the southern coastline of South Uist before crossing the causeway to Eriskay. Once on Eriskay follow the signs for the Sound of Barra Ferry which takes you through the village and to the ferry terminal where there is parking and a toilet.

Viewpoint 1 – Prince Charlies Beach

- **Lat/Long**: 57.070470, -7.3075583
- **what3words**: ///unlimited.parked.splendid
- **Grid Ref**: NF784102
- **Postcode**: HS8 5JN

Accessibility

Measuring only 2.5 by 1.5 miles, the Isle of Eriskay is easily explored on foot with access to all the viewpoints via single track road.

Best time of year/day

Eriskay is a beautiful place and looks incredible under bright summer skies, which illuminate the turquoise water that surrounds the island; it is also stunning in the winter, where it takes on a more unforgiving appearance, hunkered down against the Atlantic gales. Prince Charlies Beach is a classic sunset location.

Above: Prince Charlie's Beach from the south. Fujifilm X–T2, 18–55mm f/2.8–f/4, ISO 200, 60s at f/8. Aug.

Top: stormy weather approaching Barra. Fujifilm X–T2, 55–200mm f/3.5–f/4.8, ISO 200, 1/1700s at f/8. Mar.
Above: shells along the tideline on Prince Charlie's Beach. Fujifilm X–T1, 18–55mm f/2.8–f/4, ISO 200, 1/350s at f/8. Dec.

The turquoise sea off the coast of Eriskay. Fujifilm X–T2, 18–55mm f/2.8–f/4, ISO 200, 60s at f/8. Aug.

1 ERISKAY

Red-roofed house at Baile. Fujifilm X–T2, 18–55mm f/2.8–f/4, ISO 200, 1/1000s at f/8. Mar.

Viewpoint 2 – The village ♿

As you make your way north towards the main village, there are a number of smaller sandy bays which offer a few opportunities depending on the level of the tide, however, they are not as immediately appealing as Prince Charlies beach. The road passes two cemeteries which have an idyllic outlook and on a summers day it is a delight just to stroll through the village passing sheep and maybe even Eriskay ponies. It is well worth following the road through the village and past the shop, before it doubles back on itself and climbs up to a high point overlooking the island. Down below is the football pitch of Eriskay FC; surely the most beautiful setting for a game in Scotland. There are also great views from here across to South Uist and to Barra. The road descends back to down to the ferry terminal.

Top: *an Eriskay pony. Fujifilm X–T2, 55–200mm f/3.5–f/4.8, ISO 200, 1/125s at f/4.4. Aug.* **Above**: *Hebridean sheep. Fujifilm X–T1, 55–200mm f/3.5–f/4.8, ISO 200, 1/550s at f/4.8. Dec.*

Opposite: *the home of Eriskay F.C, Fujifilm X–T2, 18–55mm f/2.8–f/4, ISO 200, 1/750s at f/6.4. Mar.*

Gables of an old crofthouse on Vatersay. Fujifilm X–T2, 18–55mm f/2.8–f/4, ISO 200, 1/120s at f/8. Jul.

OUTER HEBRIDES FAR SOUTH

Looking over Barra and Vatersay from the the Virgin Mary and Child Statue on Heabhal. Fujifilm X–T2, 18–55mm f/2.8–f/4, ISO 200, 1/550s at f/8. Jul.

BARRA

BARRA – INTRODUCTION

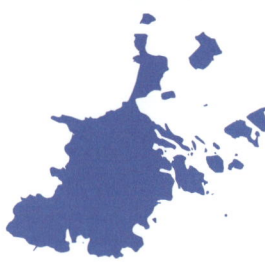

The island of Barra is the southernmost inhabited isle of the Outer Hebrides, except for Vatersay which it is joined to by a causeway. It is often called "The Hebrides in Miniature" and it is a very apt description for the diminutive island which seems to encompass all that is excellent about the Hebridean landscape. On the western side of the island you have the typically beautiful white sand beaches with Atlantic rollers breaking on the shore. In the centre of the island you have lofty peaks which provide fantastic views out to sea, particularly to the south across Vatersay and to the uninhabited isles of Sandray, Pabbay, Mingulay and Barra Head. Then there is the east coast of Barra, which is a much rockier landscape with villages tucked into bays and long open views across the sea to the distant hills on Rum and Skye. All on an island which you could drive around easily in a day, but spend a lifetime photographing.

The town of Castlebay is the bustling heart of Barra providing all the services that the island needs and where you can stock up at the supermarket and community shop for your trip. If you have come from the mainland you are likely to have arrived in Castlebay by the Caledonian MacBraybe ferry from Oban; a wonderful (but long!) journey in itself. As it skirts the northern tip of Vatersay, you get a tantalising glimpse of that islands wonderful beaches to the south and you will also pass Kisimul Castle, which is perched on a rock in the bay in an altogether beautiful setting. However dramatic this arrival is to Barra, it is still not as unique as arriving by air where the scheduled landing is actually on a beach. It is worth visiting the airport at Tràigh Mhor in the north of the island just to watch the twin prop plane landing on the sand. The view from the plane on a clear day must be incredible!

There is much to experience on Barra and there is an abundance of photographic potential throughout the island. It also really does give a fantastic introduction to the Outer Hebrides particularly if you are island-hopping your way north through the Western Isles.

How to get to Barra

You can get a ferry to Barra from the island of Eriskay which takes 40 minutes. Vehicle reservations are recommended.

Ferry
The main route to Barra is by CalMac ferry from Oban, on the mainland. The crossing takes 4 hours 45 minutes.

Air
You can fly to Barra International Airport from Glasgow. Flights are usually daily, depending on weather and cost just over £80 and take 1 hr 15 mins. Details and booking at: *loganair.co.uk*

Previous spread: a kick-about on the beach at Cleat. Fujifilm X–T2, 18–55mm f/2.8–f/4, ISO 200, 1/180s at f/8. Jul.

BARRA	
Scottish Gaelic	Eilean Bharraigh (named after Saint Finbarr of Cork).
Area	23 sq mi (60 sq km).
Length/breadth	8 × 5.5 miles.
Highest Elevation	Heaval, 383m (1,257ft).
Owned by	Private and Crown.
Population	1,174
Largest settlement(s)	Castlebay (full range of services), Ardmhor.
Vehicles allowed	Yes
Car/Bike rental	Bike Uist, Uist Bike Hire, Lasgair Bike Hire, Barra Bike Hire or in Stornoway. Car hire: *carhire-hebrides.co.uk*
Public transport	Yes. Bus timetable at *cne-siar.gov.uk*
Day trips from mainland?	No
Internet/mobile phone coverage	Broadband. 3G/4G dependent on carrier. Poor or no reception away from main towns.
Power	Grid and Wind.
Island website(s)	*explore-isle-of-barra.co.uk* • *isleofbarra.com* • *visitouterhebrides.co.uk* *visitscotland.com* • *scotland.org.uk* • *undiscoveredscotland.co.uk*
Festivals/Events	Fèis Bharraigh & BarraFest (July), Barra & Vatersay Fishing Competition (July) Barrathon (July). More at *visitouterhebrides.co.uk/whats-on* and *hebevents.com*
Accommodation	A good selection of hotels, B&Bs and self-catering cottages. *explore-isle-of-barra.co.uk/accommodation-places-to-stay* • *isleofbarra.com/accomodation* *barra-accommodation.co.uk* • *visitouterhebrides.co.uk/our-islands/barra/ accommodation*. For details of camping and facilities for motorhomes visit: *isleofbarra.com/camping.htm*
Provisions/Eating Out	There is a small selection of restaurants in Castlebay and the beautifully situated Isle of Barra Hotel to the north • *explore-isle-of-barra.co.uk/places-to-eat* There are cafes, supermarkets and a post office in Castlebay. Bùth Bharraigh is a community social enterprise offering produce and crafts. Barra Distillery has a shop.
Wildlife	Golden eagles puffins, guillemots, and kittiwakes nest on the high sheer cliffs, whilst oystercatchers and plovers. Seals, dolphins, harbour porpoise and several species of whales.
Night Sky Bortle Scale	Class 1.

LOCATIONS

1. Castlebay and Heabhal **260**
2. The West Coast **264**
3. North Barra **270**
4. The East Coast **278**

Maps

- OS Landranger Map 31 (1:50 000) Barra & South Uist, Vatersay & Eriskay

1 CASTLEBAY AND HEABHAL

At the foot of Heabhal is Castlebay, the bustling heart of Barra providing all the services that the island needs. If you have come from the mainland you are likely to have arrived in Castlebay by ferry; a wonderful journey in itself. The village is named after the ancestral seat of the clan MacNeil, Kisimul Castle, which is perched on a rock in the bay to the south in an altogether beautiful setting. Castlebay featured in the 1949 film Whisky Galore, standing in for Eriskay where the events took place and was also the inspiration for the village of Kiltoch in Tintin and the Black Isle.

What to shoot and viewpoints

Viewpoint 1 – Kisimul Castle ♿

Castlebay's main focal point is the photogenic Kisimul Castle, sitting in the bay and literally being what the village is known for. It was first occupied in the mid–16th century and even has its own fresh water wells. With its high walls and access only by boat you could imagine it being a pretty impregnable fortress for the MacNeils of Barra. It's a famous location and Tintin fans will be familiar with it as the inspiration for Craig Dhui castle in Tintin and the Black Isle where it housed the ferocious beast Ranko. There are plenty of spots to photograph it from along the road leading to the ferry terminal with on street parking normally available. The small jetty offers the opportunity to get low down at the waters edge and create an interesting foreground. »

How to get here

The main ferry to Barra from Oban on the mainland lands in Castlebay, so unless you have come by air or on the the ferry from Eriskay it is likely you will have arrived in Castlebay. It sits at the southern end of the rind road around Barra. Viewpoint 1 is accessed from the roadside within the village. To get to Viewpoint 2, head east from Castlebay and up the hill. At the crest of the hill, a small car park is located on the right hand side behind a modern house.

Viewpoint 1 – Kisimul Castle

Lat/Long:	56.954388, -7.4863795
what3words:	///glimmers.overtones.snares
Grid Ref:	NL666981
Postcode:	HS9 5XA

Viewpoint 2 – Heabhal

- **Lat/Long**: 56.960036, -7.4663724
- **what3words**: ///grownup.overpaid.squashes
- **Grid Ref**: NL678987
- **Postcode**: HS9 5UH

Accessibility

Kisimul Castle is easily viewed from the main street in Castlebay and is readily accessible. Heabhal is short but quite a steep walk and should be well within the capabilities of fit walkers.

Best time of year/day

Kisimul Castle works at most times of the year, however, it looks fantastic at sunset with the low sun catching its walls and the beaches on the Uidh peninsula. Heabhal is a great summer sunset location, but would work equally well at dawn. The view to the south is best photographed on a day with good visibility.

Above: Kisimul Castle from the shoreline at Castlebay (VP1). Fujifilm X–T2, 18–55mm f/2.8–f/4, ISO 200, 1/170s at f/8. Jul.

1 CASTLEBAY AND HEABHAL

Detail of the Virgin Mary and Child Statue on Heabhal (VP2). Fujifilm X–E3, 55–200mm f/3.5–f/4.8, ISO 200, 1/1700s at f/4.4. Jul.

Viewpoint 2 – Heabhal

The hill of Heabhal rises steeply behind Barra and its relatively low height of 383m belies its status as a fine viewpoint offering views over Castlebay, Vatersay and the remote islands to the south. It is also famous for the statue of the Virgin Mary and Child located about two thirds of the way up. To reach the statue head left at the exit of the car park and look for a stile on the roadside. From here a faint path weaves its way up steep slopes and some boggy ground. Fit walkers will reach the statue in about half an hour. The views gradually open up providing one of the most popular Hebridean scenes; Castlebay and Kisimul Castle sheltered by the Uidh peninsula and a succession of islands disappearing off into the distance in the south.

Looking over Castlebay from the the Virgin Mary and Child Statue on Heabhal (VP2). Fujifilm X–T2, 18–55mm f/2.8–f/4, ISO 200, 1/550s at f/8. Jul.

2 THE WEST COAST

Barra is known as the Hebrides in miniature and the west coast has a series of beaches which would be standouts on any Hebridean island. A drive north up the A888 will have you desperate to stop and explore, with rugged heather clad hills diving down to white sandy shores and rocky headlands. There are a number of beaches along the coastline and all are attractive for photography in their own distinct way.

What to shoot and viewpoints

Viewpoint 1 – Bàgh Halaman

The first beach you reach when heading north form Castlebay is Bàgh Halaman at the village of Tangasdale. It is a super beach with a lovely approach through the machair and over the marram topped dunes which catch the light beautifully at sunset. The sand along the tideline is steeply sloping giving rise to some cracking breakers right along the shoreline which glow with a lovely translucent tone. A scramble up onto the rocks at the eastern end provides a fantastic view back along the beach and it is possible to combine all the elements (dunes, machair, sand, sea, rock and hill) which make up the quintessential Hebridean beach scene in one image. »

A well-fed sheep in the machair at Bàgh Halaman (VP1). Fujifilm X–E3, 55–200mm f/3.5–f/4.8, ISO 200, 1/340s at f/5. Jul.

Opposite top: the dunes of Bàgh Halaman. Fujifilm X–T2, 18–55mm f/2.8–f/4, ISO 200, 1/400s at f/8. Jul. Bottom: crashing waves along the shore of Bàgh Halaman, Fujifilm X–T2, 18–55mm f/2.8–f/4, ISO 200, 1/450s at f/8. Jul.

How to get here

It is difficult to get lost on Barra with the ring road linking most of the island. To reach the beaches on the west coast, head north form Castlebay on the A888. There is plentiful parking at all of these beaches.

Viewpoint 1 – Bàgh Halaman

- **Lat/Long**: 56.970554, -7.5167360
- **what3words**: ///nudge.nutrients.bulges
- **Grid Ref**: NF6490011
- **Postcode**: HS9 5XW

Viewpoint 2 – Tràigh Hamara and Tràigh Tuath

- **Lat/Long**: 56.991816, -7.5081014
- **what3words**: ///strategy.montage.skewing
- **Grid Ref**: NF656024
- **Postcode**: HS9 5XT

Viewpoint 3 – Cleat

- **Lat/Long**: 57.014182, -7.4927744
- **what3words**: ///crimson.gilding.lunching
- **Grid Ref**: NF667048
- **Postcode**: HS9 5XX

Accessibility

All the beaches are easily accessible. Bàgh Halaman requires a short walk over grazing land and through the machair, however, faint paths will guide you towards the beach. Tràigh Hamara and Tràigh Tuath require a bit of scrambling over bouldery slopes.

Best time of year/day

As these beaches are on the west side of Barra they make ideal locations for sunset. Tràigh Hamara and Tràigh Tuath are best experienced at low tide, as at high tide much of the sandy areas are covered.

2 THE WEST COAST

Machair detail, Fujifilm X–E3, 55–200mm f/3.5–f/4.8, ISO 200, 1/450s at f/5.6. Jul.

Top: sunset from the machair on Bàgh Halaman (VP1), Fujifilm X–T2, 18–55mm f/2.8–f/4, ISO 200, 1/6s at f/8. Jul.

Clover in the machair. Fujifilm X–E3, 55–200mm f/3.5–f/4.8, ISO 200, 1/140s at f/8. Jul.

Looking north from the rocky area between Tràigh Tuath and Tràigh Hamara. Fujifilm X–T2, 18–55mm f/2.8–f/4, ISO 200, 1/13s at f/8. Jul.

Viewpoint 2 – Tràigh Hamara and Tràigh Tuath

Heading north from Tangasdale the road is sandwiched between the flanks of Beinn Mhartainn and the beaches of Tràigh Hamara and Tràigh Tuath. There are a couple of lay-bys which provide good spots to stop and scramble down the rocky slopes to these wonderful beaches. The view southwest from Tràigh Hamara is particularly attractive, with a graceful curve sand emphasised by the rolling waves breaking on the shoreline. Tràigh Tuath is not recommended for exploring, as south of the stream there is an area of quicksand, however, it is possible to experience the charms of this beach from the north. »

Looking south along the shoreline towards Tràigh Tuath (VP2). Fujifilm X–T2, 18–55mm f/2.8–f/4, ISO 200, 1/8s at f/8. Jul.

2 THE WEST COAST

Turquoise sea off the coast at Cleat (VP3). Fujifilm X–T2, 18–55mm f/2.8–f/4, ISO 200, 1/550s at f/8. Jul.

Viewpoint 3 – Cleat

As the road curves inland, a minor road branches off to the north just after Cuidhir. Follow this road north and you reach the crofting settlement of Cleat nestled on the shoulder of Beinn Chilad. The road terminates at a rocky shore, however, the best beach is located a short hop over the dunes to the east. Probably my favourite beach on Barra, this glorious spot (unnamed on the OS map) has a wonderful calm and remote feel. The best views of it are from the western end, where you can frame the whole beach and the hill of Ben Chliad. There are also some great rocky outcrops at the western end which can provide a great contrast against the pure white sand.

Top left: flowers above the shore at Cleat (VP3). Fujifilm X–T2, 18–55mm f/2.8–f/4, ISO 200, 1/210s at f/8. Jul.

Opposite: waves breaking on the northern part of Tràigh Tuath (VP2). Fujifilm X–T2, 18–55mm f/2.8–f/4, ISO 200, 1/10s at f/8. Jul.

Old caravan in the dunes at Cleat. Fujifilm X–T2, 18–55mm f/2.8–f/4, ISO 200, 1/240s at f/9. Jul.

3 NORTH BARRA

The north of Barra really highlights the great variety of photographing opportunities on this small island, encompassing extensive tidal sand flats, a huge dune-backed beach, a harbour and even an airport.

It is a great area to spend the day, with plenty to shoot and an excellent cafe in the airport for lunch.

What to shoot and viewpoints

Viewpoint 1 – The Airport ♿

Whilst not a typical landscape photography subject, you can't help but make time to shoot the image of the Twin Otter plane from Glasgow landing on the sans of Tràigh Mhor at Barra International Airport. The only airport with a scheduled landing on a beach, Barra Airport is totally unique and is used by over 8,500 passengers a year with more than 1500 take offs and landings. The wide sandy beach, once only famed for its cockles now has three runways (one more than Heathrow!) which ensure that planes can take off and land into the wind. The best place to view the planes coming in to land is from the barrier at the car park, and you will have a great spot to watch as it pulls right up to the terminal building. Flight times are available at: hial.co.uk/barra-airport, however, they can be delayed so it's best to go and check with the friendly staff in the building. »

A small plane on the beach at Barra International Airport (VP1). Fujifilm X–T2, 18–55mm f/2.8–f/4, ISO 200, 1/750s at f/8. Jul.

How to get here

From the A888 ring road, take the road north at Bayherivagh signposted to the airport. The road skirts around the shoreline of Tràigh Mhor. Park in the airport car park. For Eoligarry, head north from the airport keeping right at the junction after the school. After a few minutes you will reach a car park at the harbour. From here you can access both the harbour and the beach.

Viewpoint 1 – The Airport & Viewpoint 2 – Tràigh Eais

- **Lat/Long**: 57.025254, -7.4496066
- **what3words**: ///mavericks.gallons.privately
- **Grid Ref**: NF694058
- **Postcode**: HS9 5YR

Viewpoint 3 – Eoligarry

- **Lat/Long**: 57.041765, -7.4212403
- **what3words**: ///desire.dumplings.winds
- **Grid Ref**: NF713075
- **Postcode**: HS9 5YD

Viewpoint 4 – Crannag

- **Lat/Long**: 57.013030, -7.4290892
- **what3words**: ///protect.viewer.exact
- **Grid Ref**: NF706044
- **Postcode**: HS9 5YB

Accessibility

All locations are essentially roadside and easily accessed. Do not attempt to cross Tràigh Mhor when the wind sock is flying and beware of the tide as it can race in very fast. Tràigh Eais is a short steep walk over the dunes but shouldn't pose any problems. Crannag is roadside.

Best time of year/day

Tràigh Eais is a classic west-facing sunset location, especially coupled with a big swell. If you want to catch the plane landing or taking off, consult the timetable on the Highlands and Islands Airports website. It is unlikely they will land in foggy conditions, so it is best left to a clear day. Tràigh Sgurabhal is fine in all conditions and even on overcast days the water has a wonderful glow to it. Crannag is east facing and good for sunrise.

Above: watching the plane arriving on the beach (VP1). Fujifilm X–E3, 55–200mm f/3.5–f/4.8, ISO 200, 1/1000s at f/6.4. Jul. *Below*: the LoganAir plane from Glasgow on the sand at Barra International Airport. Fujifilm X–E3, 55–200mm f/3.5–f/4.8, ISO 200, 1/1000s at f/6.4. Jul.

3. NORTH BARRA

Looking north along Tràigh Eais from the dunes (VP2), Fujifilm X–T2, 18–55mm f/2.8–f/4, ISO 200, 1/680s at f/8. Jul.

Viewpoint 2 – Tràigh Eais

To the west of the airport, is the magnificent beach, Tràigh Eais. Stretching for over a mile, this beach has all the ingredients needed for a classic Hebridean beach. A path opposite the entrance to the airport leads straight through the dunes. The rocks at either end are also worth a visit and the headland at the south, as well as the dunes, provides a wonderful elevated views of the beach. »

The dunes at Tràigh Eais, Fujifilm X–T2, 18–55mm f/2.8–f/4, ISO 200, 1/800s at f/8. Jul.

Opposite: Exploring the pier at Eoligarry (VP3).

3 NORTH BARRA

Above: rainclouds gather over Cidhe Eòlaigearraidh (VP3). Fujifilm X–T2, 18–55mm f/2.8–f/4, ISO 200, 1/450s at f/8. Jul. **Left**: *Machair above the beach at Tràigh Sgurabhal (VP3). Fujifilm X–T2, 18–55mm f/2.8–f/4, ISO 200, 1/480s at f/8. Jul.*

Viewpoint 3 – Eoligarry

North of the airport is the scattered settlement of Eoligarry which occupies an idyllic location looking out across turquoise waters to the islands of Fuday and Eriskay. There is a small harbour, which will be of interest to those who enjoy studies of fishing paraphernalia such as creels, buoys, nets and the like. North of the pier is a large sandy beach, Tràigh Sgurabhal, which backs onto a lovely area of machair. At low tide you may see an area of oyster beds. »

Oyster trestles at Eoligarry. Fujifilm X–T2, 18–55mm f/2.8–f/4, ISO 200, 1/500s at f/8. Jul.

Opposite: *Eoligarry harbour. Fujifilm X–T2, 18–55mm f/2.8–f/4, ISO 200, 1/400s at f/8. Jul.*

3 NORTH BARRA

Red roofed house at Crannag. Fujifilm X–T2, 18–55mm f/2.8–f/4, ISO 200, 1/450s at f/8. Jul.

Viewpoint 4 – Crannag ♿

This small village is located just off the A888 ring road on the way to the airport and is clustered around a small sandy beach with a red roofed house perched in the most idyllic of locations on a small headland. It is also home to a wonderful old decaying boat which can make for some great detail studies. There is a small area to park on the minor road heading to Ardmhor next to a barn, from here head north through the village and onto the sand. The best views of the cottage are from the headland to the west. You may see the flight from Glasgow coming in to land on the beach to the north

The old boat at Crannag. Fujifilm X–T2, 18–55mm f/2.8–f/4, ISO 200, 1/500s at f/8. Jul.

Above: *textures in the old boat (VP4). Fujifilm X–T2, 18–55mm f/2.8–f/4, ISO 200, 1/320s at f/8. Jul.*

Below left: the wee house on the promontory at Crannag. Fujifilm X–T2, 18–55mm f/2.8–f/4, ISO 200, 1/680s at f/8. Jul.
Below right: a good day for drying the washing. Fujifilm X–E3, 55–200mm f/3.5–f/4.8, ISO 200, 1/480s at f/6.4. Jul.

4 EAST COAST

The East Coast of Barra is very different to the west. Gone are the sweeping Atlantic beaches, replaced with intimate rocky coves and tidal islands. There are numerous settlements along the east coast all linked by a sinuous road which meanders past small harbours somewhat reminiscent of the Golden Road in Harris. If you are lucky enough to visit on a clear day there are splendid views across the Sea of The Hebrides to Skye and Rum. The only difficulty along this stretch of coast is finding enough suitable places to stop and park.

What to shoot and viewpoints

Earsary and Breivig ♿

As you descend from the shoulder of Heabhal coming east from Castlebay, the villages of Breivig and Earsary come into view. These small villages are perched along the shoreline and the intricate bays with jetties and harbours have a lot to offer the coastal photographer. Stacked creels, ropes and buoys can make for some lovely studies and the old boat at Earsary is great as a foreground to the view up the coast or for detail studies of its cracked and peeling paint. The white house beside the road at Earsary is perched in a fantastic location, creating a very pretty and typically Hebridean scene. Parking is scarce in this area so in some ways it is easier to walk along the coast road rather than drive between spots you may have seen from the car.

Top: a seat with a view at Earsary. Fujifilm X–T2, 18–55mm f/2.8–f/4, ISO 200, 1/9s at f/8. Jul. **Above**: creels at the roadside. Fujifilm X–T2, 18–55mm f/2.8–f/4, ISO 200, 1/50s at f/4.5. Jul.

Opposite top: crofthouse on the corner at Earsary. Fujifilm X–T2, 14mm f/2.8, ISO 200, 1/450s at f/8. Jul. **Bottom**: one of the many rocky bays along the east coast. Fujifilm X–T2, 14mm f/2.8, ISO 200, 1/75s at f/8. Jul.

How to get here

To reach the east coast, head east from Castlebay on the A888. There is limited parking, however, some of the larger passing places can be used with care, ensuring that you leave enough room for them to be used. Approaching Earsary from the west you will pass a small white cottage on the right before a bend, and there is space to carefully pull off the road beside the lamppost.

Earsary and Breivig

- **Lat/Long:** 56.968146, -7.4254230
- **what3words:** ///careless.dancer.index
- **Grid Ref:** NL704994
- **Postcode:** HS9 5UR

Accessibility

These locations are easily accessible along the road or on footpaths.

Best time of year/day

As these are predominately east facing these locations would be excellent sunrise spots, however, the detail studies can be photographed well under flat light.

Next spread: an old boat in the bay at Earsary. Fujifilm X–T2, 14mm f/2.8, ISO 200, 1/40s at f/5.6. Jul.

VATERSAY – INTRODUCTION

The name Vatersay means Water Island and it is easy to see why, with its convoluted coastline which seems to constantly double back on itself, you are never far away from the sea as you travel around the island.

The peninsula of Uidh reaches out to the east of Vatersay towards the uninhabited isle of Maòl Domhnaich, and provides a fantastic view back to Castlebay, with the town and castle huddled around the waters edge at the foot of Heabhal. A single track road winds its way across the peninsula which offers a number of diverse photographic opportunities including ruined croft houses and some glorious Hebridean beaches which, more often than not, you will have all to yourself.

As you travel round the shoulder of Heisabhal Beag, a truly wondrous view opens up, the beach at Bàgh Bhatarsaigh (Vatersay Bay). One of the real gems of Vatersay, this beach is a sheltered crescent of white sand. Together with Traigh Siar over the dunes, this location offers a great walk and all that a seascape photographer could ask for. The community hall also has a great cafe, so make sure you walk enough to justify a cake or two! Further to the south is another lovely beach and the abandoned settlement of village Eòrasdail which sits in a remote location looking out to the inhabited island of Sandray.

How to get to Vatersay

A causeway links Barra and Vatersay.

Looking across to Sandray from Bàgh a' Deas. Fujifilm X–T2, 18–55mm f/2.8–f/4, ISO 200, 1/550s at f/8. Jul.

VATERSAY	
Scottish Gaelic	Bhatarsaigh (Water Island).
Area	3.75 sq mi (9.7 sq km).
Length/breadth	3 × 3.5 miles.
Highest Elevation	Heiseabhal Mòr, 190m (623ft).
Owned by	Private and community owned.
Population	90
Largest settlement(s)	Baile Bhatarsaigh.
Vehicles allowed	Yes
Car/Bike rental	Bike Uist, Uist Bike Hire, Lasgair Bike Hire, Barra Bike Hire or in Stornoway. Car hire: carhire-hebrides.co.uk
Public transport	Yes. Bus timetable at cne-siar.gov.uk
Day trips from mainland?	No
Internet/mobile phone coverage	Broadband. 3G/4G dependent on carrier. Poor or no reception away from main towns.
Power	Grid and renewables.
Island website(s)	visitouterhebrides.co.uk/our-islands/barra/vatersay • visitouterhebrides.co.uk visitscotland.com • scotland.org.uk • undiscoveredscotland.co.uk outaboutscotland.com/isle-of-vatersay
Festivals/Events	visitouterhebrides.co.uk/whats-on and hebevents.com
Accommodation	Motorhome parking places and wild camping at the community hall (showers and toilets).
Provisions/Eating Out	Vatersay cafe, community hall
Wildlife	Terns, guillemots and black-headed gulls, otters, golden eagles, seals, dolphins, harbour porpoise and several species of whales. Bonnie Prince Charlie's Flower.
Night Sky Bortle Scale	Class 1.

LOCATIONS

1. The Gables 286
2. The beaches 288
3. Bàgh Bhatarsaigh 291
4. Traigh Siar 291
5. Bàgh a' Deas 292
6. Eòrasdail 294

Maps

- OS Landranger Map 31 (1:50 000) Barra & South Uist, Vatersay & Eriskay

Previous spread: An old boat on the shore at Bàgh Bhatarsaigh. Fujifilm X–T2, 18–55mm f/2.8–f/4, ISO 200, 1/480s at f/8. Jul.

1 VATERSAY

What to shoot and viewpoints

Viewpoint 1 – The Gables

One of the most unique features along the road is the remains of a croft house roughly half way along. Whilst these ruins are always a poignant reminder of a lost way of life this one feels especially sad, perhaps because it looks out to the bustling town of Castlebay seemingly emphasising its loneliness. The two gables of the house are still standing and look in fine condition with chimney pots intact and it is in a grand spot, sitting above a luminous blue sea which adds an almost otherworldly quality to the view. There is a large passing place on the road just east of the ruins and it is possible to park here providing you allow enough space for others. It's a quite a tight spot to frame the house, so a wide angle lens may be useful here. »

How to get here

After the causeway which links Barra and Vatersay, turn right following the sign for Vatersay. When the roads forks at the bus shelter, head left towards the steep slopes of Heisabhal Mòr. The road now runs east along the southern shore of Bàgh Cornaig. As you pass a house on the left the road heads inland, at the next junction take the road on the left and follow as it winds along the peninsula. The first viewpoint is reached after a bend in the road at a small jetty. Return to the main road and turn left, following the road onwards until you reach the community centre on the left. Further on at the village of Vatersay there are spaces for parking just prior to the beach.

Viewpoint 1 – The Gables

Lat/Long:	56.934396, -7.5060308
what3words:	///trucks.vampire.magazines
Grid Ref:	NL652960
Postcode:	HS9 5YN

The gables of an old house at Uidh with Castlebay on Barra beyond. Fujifilm X–T2, 18–55mm f/2.8–f/4, ISO 200, 1/280s at f/8. Jul.

Left: Straight-on view of the right gable. Fujifilm X–T2, 18–55mm f/2.8–f/4, ISO 200, 1/400s at f/8. Jul.

Opposite: Oblique view of the left gable. Fujifilm X–T2, 18–55mm f/2.8–f/4, ISO 200, 1/200s at f/8. Jul.

1 VATERSAY

Viewpoint 2 – The Beaches

At the end of Uidh peninsula are a string of fine, sheltered beaches which are ideal for a swim after a hard day of (summer) photography! All of theses beaches have crystal clear turquoise waters and look back across to Barra. Ideal for sunset and sunrise, they still look fantastic on a grey day with the turquoise waters almost appearing to glow under cloudy skies. The Uidh road terminates at a bus turning circle and it is possible to park just off this, making sure there is still plenty of room for the bus to turn. The first beach is located to the west of this via a short stroll across the grass down to the shoreline. The other beaches are located to the east; from the parking area head down to a gate and onto the first beach, a beautiful dune backed crescent of white sand. From the east end of this beach head up over the headland and follow the path along to another small beach which at low tide connects the island of Uineasan to Uidh. »

Looking east along the Uidh peninsula to the beaches. Fujifilm X–T2, 18–55mm f/2.8–f/4, ISO 200, 1/950s at f/5.6. Jul.

Viewpoint 2 – The Beaches

- **Lat/Long**: 56.933976, -7.4972022
- **what3words**: ///scribble.commutes.parting
- **Grid Ref**: NL657959
- **Postcode**: HS9 5YN

Viewpoint 3 – Bàgh Bhatarsaigh & Viewpoint 4 – Traigh Siar

- **Lat/Long**: 56.927137, -7.5363145
- **what3words**: ///refusals.lobbed.receiving
- **Grid Ref**: NL633954
- **Postcode**: HS9 5YW

Above right: collie watching the cows on the beach at Uidh. Fujifilm X–T2, 18–55mm f/2.8–f/4, ISO 200, 1/340s at f/8. Jul.
Opposite left: looking across to Castlebay and cloud-capped Heabhal from Uidh. Fujifilm X–T2, 18–55mm f/2.8–f/4, ISO 200, 1/480s at f/8. Jul. Right: a ruined cottage at Uidh. Fujifilm X–T2, 18–55mm f/2.8–f/4, ISO 200, 1/340s at f/8. Jul.

1 VATERSAY

Bàgh Bhatarsaigh from the south. Fujifilm X–T2, 18–55mm f/2.8–f/4, ISO 200, 1/350s at f/10. Jul.

Viewpoint 3 – Bàgh Bhatarsaigh

From the car park at the community hall, a track across the machair gives access to the beach. In summer the machair gives a great foreground to the beach and is also excellent for intimate landscape shots of the wildflowers. The beach itself is a typical Hebridean sandy beach, and is a popular spot for swimming on sunny days. As you head to the southern end of the beach there is an old boat which is gradually succumbing to the harsh climate and makes for a fascinating study in decay with old peeling paint and rusting ironwork. At the southern end of the beach a road leads into the village of Vatersay and eventually back round to the community centre. There is a wonderful yellow boat next to an old croft house which makes for another interesting study.

Viewpoint 4 – Traigh Siar

Traigh Siar is located a short hop over the dunes from the community hall and offers a real contrast to Bàgh Bhatarsaigh. It is a dramatic beach on a stormy day with waves crashing upon the stony shore providing some great movement for long exposure shots. It is a beach with a sad history. In September 1853, the Annie Jane, a three-masted migrant ship bound for Montreal from Liverpool ran aground offshore in a storm. The ship broke apart on the rocks and 450 people were cast into the sea. Despite the locals rescue attempts, only a few people survived. The bodies washed up on the beach and were buried in a mass grave due to the lack of timber for coffins. A memorial on the dunes marks this dark day in the history of Vatersay. »

Above middle: *looking west to Bàgh Bhatarsaigh from Beinn Chuidhir. Fujifilm X–T2, 18–55mm f/2.8–f/4, ISO 200, 1/900s at f/8. Jul.* **Above**: *yellow boat at Bàgh Bhatarsaigh. Fujifilm X–T2, 18–55mm f/2.8–f/4, ISO 200, 1/140s at f/5.6. Jul.*

Opposite: *an old boat at Bàgh Bhatarsaigh with Heabhal on Barra in the background. Fujifilm X–T2, 18–55mm f/2.8–f/4, ISO 200, 1/400s at f/8. Jul.*

1 VATERSAY

Stormy sea at Traigh Siar. Fujifilm X–T1, 18–55mm f/2.8–f/4, ISO 200, 1s at f/8. Dec.

Paddling at Bàgh Bhatarsaigh. Fujifilm X–T2, 18–55mm f/2.8–f/4, ISO 200, 1/640s at f/8. Jul.

Viewpoint 5 – Bàgh a' Deas

From the village of Vatersay head west towards Bàgh Bhatarsaigh, once past a cattle grid take the track on the right which leads out across the machair to the south. After 10 minutes you will arrive at Bàgh a' Deas, a lovely sheltered sandy beach which provides a great view to the rugged and uninhabited island of Sandray. You are likely to find cows here, sunning themselves on the beach or grazing on the machair and they can add a real charm to your images. »

Viewpoint 5 – Bàgh a' Deas & Viewpoint 6 – Eòrasdail

- Lat/Long: 56.919185, -7.5360180
- what3words: ///darts.chart.hunter
- Grid Ref: NL632945
- Postcode: HS9 5YU

Accessibility

All the viewpoints are easily accessible for walkers and you can really make these walks as easy as you like. Uineasan can be boggy in places and there are a few steep slopes getting to and from the beaches, however, these can be bypassed. Be careful with the tides at Uineasan as it is possible to get either stranded or very wet feet crossing back to the peninsula. The route to Eòrasdail can be very boggy so wellies or walking boots are recommended. The paths are faint and map reading skills are recommended in inclement weather.

Opposite: old tractor on the way to Eòrasdail. Fujifilm X–T2, 18–55mm f/2.8–f/4, ISO 200, 1/420s at f/8. Jul.

1 VATERSAY

Viewpoint 6 – Eòrasdail

These days the island of Vatersay is the southernmost inhabited isle in the Outer Hebrides, but it wasn't always the case. The islands to the south supported a large and thriving population, exporting fish to Glasgow and with some locals travelling to work in the herring trade on the north east coast of Scotland. However, the lack of sheltered harbours, the problems caused by being cut off for months at time, and the loss of life of nearly half of Pabbay's men in a shipwreck, resulted in a gradual evacuation from the islands. Many residents emigrated overseas, however some stayed in the Outer Hebrides, moving to Barra and Vatersay.

In 1906 grazing land in Vatersay under the ownership of Lady Gordon Cathcart was seized by the men who subsequently came to be known as the Vatersay Raiders. These men, from Barra, Vatersay and Mingulay, struggling to find suitable land to farm invoked an ancient rite which involved sailing around an island, building a shelter and lighting a fire in a single day to claim that land for themselves. It was not looked upon favourably by the landowner and they were imprisoned in Edinburgh for their actions. However, their raid was not in vain as in 1909 the Congested Districts Board bought the island and split it into 58 crofts, some of which are still occupied today by descendants of the Vatersay Raiders.

Best time of year/day

One of the best features of this location is that it faces both east and west so can offer plenty of opportunities at both sunrise or sunset; you can even nip between the two if the sky looks more interesting in the other direction! Summer is fantastic here, especially when the machair is in bloom, however, winter is also special, especially if you have some dramatic weather on Traigh Siar. Eòrasdail is great for those misty, grey days where the haunting feel of the abandoned village can be matched by that of the weather.

Above: Machair above Bàgh a' Deas. Fujifilm X–T2, 18–55mm f/2.8–f/4, ISO 200, 1/500s at f/11. Jul.

One of the roofless crofthouses at Eòrasdail. Fujifilm X–T2, 18–55mm f/2.8–f/4, ISO 200, 1/210s at f/9. Jul.

The abandoned village of Eòrasdail was one of the places settled by the Vatersay Raiders and sits at the southern end of the island above a small pebble beach with a view to the island of Sandray. It was never connected by road and this remoteness eventually led to the homes being abandoned in the 1930s. There are a few of the buildings still standing and the atmospheric ruins provide a stark monument to the hard lives endured by the residents. In spring and summer the ruins are surrounded by wildflowers which bloom amidst the tumbledown walls of the former settlement. To get to Eòrasdail follow the same route to Bàgh a' Deas and then head south following the markers. This takes you down through some boggy land via a few stream crossings to the village itself. From here, a faint path leads up to the north and marker posts lead you back to the village.

Machair at Eòrasdail with Sandray on the horizon. Fujifilm X–T2, 18–55mm f/2.8–f/4, ISO 200, 1/450s at f/5.6. Jul.

ST KILDA

ST KILDA – INTRODUCTION

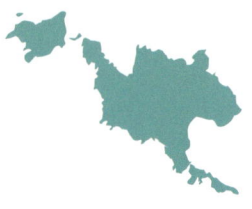

St Kilda is a special place, an archipelago of towering islands off the west coast of The Hebrides 40 miles out to sea in the wild Atlantic. Remote, hard to reach and resonant with a fascinating ancient and recent history, it is simply an unforgettable place and one that I would urge anyone to visit, the memories you make here will last a lifetime. The St Kilda archipelago includes the largest island Hirta (where you stay/visit), three smaller islands Dùn, Soay and Boreray and several sea stacks (stac).

The story of St Kilda has been the subject of many books and a good understanding of the history of the people, their culture and ultimately their heartbreaking decision to leave the island will definitely enrich your trip. The palimpsest of history, from the thousands of scattered cleitean on the hillsides to the more recent military uses are clearly revealed to the visitor but a knowledge of the peoples story and the paradox of both the harsh realities and idyllic qualities of life on St Kilda is vital to the experience.

The natural landscape of St Kilda is equally distinctive, the remains of an extinct volcano, long since sunk below the waves; the islands and sea stacks of the archipelago are both frighteningly dramatic in places and calm and tranquil in others. Birdlife dominates, with fulmars racing on the wind, piratical bonxies, the largest colony of gannets in the world and puffins strutting outside their clifftop burrows. Soay sheep, a third of the size of the sheep on the mainland, roam freely on the island. There are species only found here like the St Kilda Wren and the St Kilda Field-mouse.

It is no surprise that the islands have been awarded dual UNESCO World Heritage Site status for both the natural environment and for their cultural importance. The only one of its kind in the UK and one of only a handful worldwide. It is very rare find a place as special as St Kilda. The entire archipelago is owned and managed by the National Trust for Scotland.

How to get to St Kilda

Lat/Long: 57.811846, -8.5713100
what3words: ///mule.pounds.swooned
Grid Ref: NF 099 992

Day Trips
Getting to St Kilda by boat is thought to be an exhilarating adventure or a miserable slog depending on your propensity for seasickness. Generally most passengers are not seasick and tour operators advise the best course of action to take prior to the trip to ensure you have a comfortable crossing. Tour boats providing day trips to St Kilda sail from Lewis, Harris, Skye, South Uist and Barra, with the shortest crossing from Harris taking 2.5hours in ideal conditions. Day trips are very popular and tend to be booked months, sometimes years in advance. They are also subject to the weather and liable to cancellation or delay at the last minute.

You can take a day trip (4hrs on the island) to St Kilda with one of these tour operators.

From Harris:
Kilda Cruises (£285 per person in 2023)
kildacruises.co.uk

Sea Harris (£260 per person in 2023)
seaharris.com

From South Uist:
Uist Sea Tours (£255 per person in 2023)
uistseatours.co.uk

From Barra:
Hebridean Sea Tours (£265 per person in 2023)
hebrideanseatours.co.uk

From Skye:
Go to St Kilda (£285 per person in 2023)
gotostkilda.co.uk offer a day trips from the Isle of Skye which is connected to the mainland if you don't mind a longer boat trip and are not planning on visiting Harris.

ST KILDA	
Scottish Gaelic	Hiort.
Area	3.3 sq mi (8.5 sq km).
Length/breadth	3.2 × 2 miles.
Highest Elevation	Conachair, 430m (1,410ft).
Owned by	National Trust Scotland.
Population	The main island of Hirta is still occupied all year round by a small number of civilians working in the military base.
Largest settlement(s)	N/A
Vehicles allowed	No
Car/Bike rental	No
Public transport	No
Day trips from mainland?	Day trips from Harris, Barra and Skye.
Internet/mobile phone coverage	No
Power	Diesel generator.
Island website(s)	nts.org.uk/visit/places/st-kilda • whc.unesco.org/en/list/387 visitouterhebrides.co.uk • visitscotland.com • scotland.org.uk undiscoveredscotland.co.uk
Festivals/Events	St Kilda Challenge (June) thestkildachallenge.co.uk
Accommodation	Camping
Provisions/Eating Out	Bring your own.
Wildlife	Home to nearly 1 million seabirds, including the UK's largest colony of Atlantic puffins. Seals, dolphins, harbour porpoise and several species of whales.
Night Sky Bortle Scale	Class 1.

LOCATIONS

1 Approach from the sea **302**
2 Village bay **304**
3 Main Street **306**
4 The Gap and Conachair **310**
5 Dùn and Ruabhal **312**

Maps

- OS Explorer Map 460 (1:25 000) North Uist, St Kilda and the Flannan Islands

Previous spread: Gannets in flight off the coast of Boreray.
Fujifilm X–T2, 18–55mm f/2.8–f/4, ISO 200,
1/600s at f/5. Aug.

Overleaf: Map of St Kilda or Hirta and adjacent Islands and Stacs

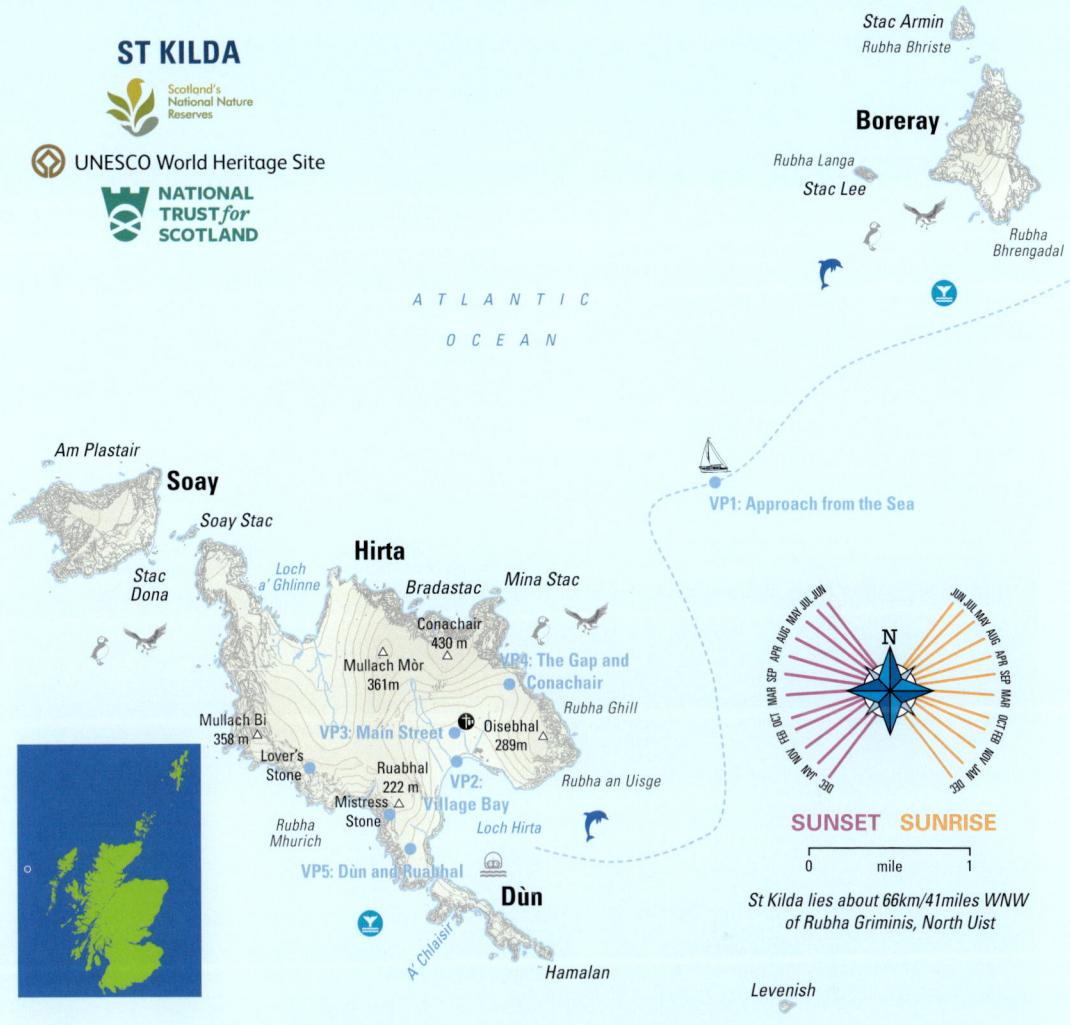

Opposite: Main Street St Kilda. Fujifilm X–T2, 18–55mm f/2.8–f/4, ISO 200, 1/480s at f/7.1. Aug.

Staying on St Kilda

If you would like more time on the island, it is also possible to camp by contacting National Trust for Scotland at: stkildainfo@nts.org.uk

The only accommodation for visitors is a small campsite on the main island of Hirta. The campsite must be pre-booked and visitors may stay for up to 5 nights. In 2023, the campsite was open from 19 April–10 August and 23 August–12 September.

It is recommend that you pack enough supplies in case the return sailing is delayed; campers have been known to be stranded on the island for a week. It is also recommended that you take metal storage containers for your food as the native St Kilda mouse is a voracious eater and will happily work its way through your food.

More information can be found at:
nts.org.uk/visit/places/st-kilda/planning-your-visit

1 ST KILDA

What to shoot and viewpoints

Viewpoint 1 – Approach from the Sea

Most boat trips to St Kilda will visit the island of Boreray and its associated sea stacks, four miles to the northwest of Hirta either on the way there or on the way back. For some it is the highlight of the trip. Boreray is a dark and brooding presence, its towering cliffs thrusting out of the sea and playing host to the largest gannet colony in the world. There is a 'lost world' feel about Boreray, one where a pterodactyl flying out from the cliffs wouldn't be entirely surprising. The sea stacks of Stac Lee and Stac an Armin rise out the water like leviathans, with their wave scoured sides circled by gannets. Photographing Boreray and the stacks on a rocking boat is tricky, make the best you can of it. You don't really want to be changing lenses out on the ocean so ideally use a lens with a good wide-angle to telephoto range. This will enable you to make images of Boreray and the stacks but also to home in on smaller details on the cliffs or the puffins which are often seen afloat at the base of the cliffs. »

The dramatic cliffs on the west of St Kilda (VP1). Fujifilm X–T2, 18–55mm f/2.8–f/4, ISO 200, 1/340s at f/5. Aug.

Accessibility

There are good paths along the Main Street and around the shoreline of Village Bay and people with limited mobility may feel most comfortable staying in these areas; there is a lot to see and many people are happy to stay within the Village soaking up the atmosphere. If you venture up above the village or towards the west the terrain becomes very rugged, pathless and steep. There are huge cliffs all around the island, however, the cliffs at The Gap are especially treacherous, with crumbling edges over a huge drop. It is recommended that you stay well back from the edge here.

The islands weather is notoriously fickle and can change in an instant, mist and cloud can descend to low levels making route finding difficult.

Best time of year/day

Day trips to St Kilda generally run from April to September. Your time on the island is not guaranteed and depends on the tides and weather. However long you have, and whatever weather conditions you are blessed or cursed with, enjoy your time on St Kilda. There really is nowhere else like it.

Above: *a gannet flies past Stac Lee off the coast of Boreray. Fujifilm X–T2, 18–55mm f/2.8–f/4, ISO 200, 1/850s at f/5. Aug.*
Below: *puffin take-off (VP1). Fujifilm X–T2, 55–200mm f/3.5–f/4.8, ISO 200, 1/950s at f/4.8. Aug.*

1 ST KILDA

Cloud cap on Boreray (VP1). Fujifilm X–T2, 18–55mm f/2.8–f/4, ISO 200, 1/2400s at f/5. Aug.

Viewpoint 2 – Village Bay

As you sail into village bay, you may feel a number of differing emotions. Excitement, definitely. Relief, perhaps that the journey is over or maybe awe at the huge hills towering over the village. You might also feel a slight sense of disappointment at the sight of the modern buildings on the island. They are not commonly shown in the tourist literature but the military buildings are just another part in the long story of the place. That said the new buildings, with their timber cladding and green roofs are much less imposing than the old ones which they have replaced. There are a number of excellent spots for photography along the bay, the beach is a lovely sweep of golden sand at low tide, and at high tide the waves break on the large boulders which line the shore. At the eastern end of

The road along Village Bay (VP2). Fujifilm X–T2, 18–55mm f/2.8–f/4, ISO 200, 1/240s at f/7.1. Aug.

Village Bay is the Feather Store, a stout two–storey building where the residents stored the feathers they used to pay rent. The view of the building towards the island of Dùn which shelters the bay is a classic. Also worth a visit are the church and the school buildings. »

Above: looking to Dùn from the boulders on the beach at high tide (VP2). Fujifilm X–T2, 18–55mm f/2.8–f/4, ISO 200, 60s at f/8. Aug.
Below: the Feather Store (VP2). Fujifilm X–T2, 18–55mm f/2.8–f/4, ISO 200, 20s at f/7.1. Aug.

1 ST KILDA

Above*: looking out the window of the Schoolhouse (VP2). Fujifilm X–T2, 18–55mm f/2.8–f/4, ISO 200, 1/240s at f/4. Aug.* ***Top right****: Gun emplacement next to the Feather Store (VP2). Fujifilm X–T2, 18–55mm f/2.8–f/4, ISO 200, 30s at f/8. Aug.* ***Bottom right****: The classroom. Fujifilm X–T2, 18–55mm f/2.8–f/4, ISO 200, 1/60s at f/4. Aug.*

Viewpoint 3 – Main Street

Walking along the main street on the island of Hirta, you can feel a palpable sense of history all around you. The houses, some restored and providing accommodation for researchers, arc gracefully around the bay at the foot of Conachair. Many of the houses have a slate plaque within them or outside marking the names of the residents. Soay sheep graze the grass in front of the houses and on a sunny day it feels like an idyllic place, on days like this you can experience how much of a difficult a decision it was to leave the island. On a day of heavy rain, perhaps not so much. Some of the buildings are not restored and their tumbledown walls provide great subjects. To the north of the village is the cemetery, with its ancient gravestones weathered by the rain, another evocative sign of the lost community of Hirta. »

Main Street from above, Fujifilm X–T2, 18–55mm f/2.8–f/4, ISO 200, 1/250s at f/8. Aug.

Opposite top*: Looking along Main Street (VP3). Fujifilm X–T2, 18–55mm f/2.8–f/4, ISO 200, 1/480s at f/7.1. Aug.* ***Bottom****: The graveyard (VP3). Fujifilm X–T2, 18–55mm f/2.8–f/4, ISO 200, 1/320s at f/5.6. Aug.*

Night falls on Main Street (VP3). Fujifilm X–T2, 18–55mm f/2.8–f/4, ISO 200, 20s at f/8. Aug.

1 ST KILDA

A cleit on the slopes above Village Bay (VP4). Fujifilm X–T2, 18–55mm f/2.8–f/4, ISO 200, 1/500s at f/7.1. Aug.

Viewpoint 4 – The Gap and Conachair

All visitors should try and make the trip up to the Gap, the name given to the bealach (pass or col) between the peaks of Conachair and Oisebhal. From the village, walk up through the cleitean and onto the open ground beyond. The cleitean are fascinating stone structures topped with turf, designed to both dry and store food and some are believed to be over 2000 years old. This higher elevation also provides a good view of the Main Street. Further on the numerous sheepfolds provide some great foreground elements. After 20/30minutes the land steepens before you appear at the Gap. It's a remarkable place, with a clear view across the sea to Boreray and the stacks. It's also a busy place, with fulmars drifting past on the updraught and bonxies patrolling the skies. From the Gap follow the cliffs northwest to the summit of Conachair where there is a fantastic view back down to Village Bay. »

Looking to Boreray from The Gap. Fujifilm X–T2, 18–55mm f/2.8–f/4, ISO 200, 1/500s at f/5.6. Aug.

Opposite top: winter feed enclosures below Conachair (VP4). Fujifilm X–T2, 18–55mm f/2.8–f/4, ISO 200, 1/350s at f/8. Aug.
Bottom: looking down to Village Bay from the slopes of Conachair (VP4). Fujifilm X–T2, 18–55mm f/2.8–f/4, ISO 200, 1/180s at f/8. Aug.

1 ST KILDA

The Mistress Stone. (VP5), Fujifilm X–T2, 18–55mm f/2.8–f/4, ISO 200, 1/220s at f/8. Aug.

Viewpoint 5 – Dùn and Ruabhal

Sheltering Village Bay from the ferocity of the Atlantic is the distinctive saw toothed ridge of the island of Dùn. It is home to a large colony of puffins and is separated from Hirta by a very small channel. Unfortunately this means that access on foot is impossible, however, there are great views to the island from the slopes of Ruabhal. From Village Bay, follow the shoreline past the Helipad and gradually ascend the grassy slopes which lead south passing a telescope and a sheep fold. There are some paths here but the going is quite steep. On the skyline is The Mistress stone, a large block of rock balanced precariously above the cliffs. Further to the north west the cliffs rise to Mullach Bi, passing the Lover's Stone. This stone juts out above the water and young men proved their worth to their future wife by standing on one leg above the gut wrenching drop. A head for heights was necessary to the St Kildans who relied on surefooted climbing to harvest the eggs and birds on the precipitous cliffs.

Top right: Soay Sheep on the slope of Ruabhal (VP5). Fujifilm X–T2, 18–55mm f/2.8–f/4, ISO 200, 1/450s at f/8. Aug.

The rugged west coast of St Kilda (VP5). Fujifilm X–T2, 18–55mm f/2.8–f/4, ISO 200, 1/300s at f/8. Aug.

Above: Bonxie on Ruabhal (VP5). Fujifilm X–T2, 55–200mm f/3.5–f/4.8, ISO 200, 1/840s at f/4.8. Aug. *Above right*: the island of Dùn from the southern edge of Ruabhal (VP5). Fujifilm X–T2, 18–55mm f/2.8–f/4, ISO 200, 1/1000s at f/5.6. Aug.

ABOUT THE AUTHOR – CHRISTOPHER SWAN

Biography

Based in Glasgow, Chris has been exploring the Hebrides since he was a young boy on family holidays. For the last five years he has devoted most of his time traveling to all the islands whilst working on this book. Originally a landscape architect, he became a full-time photographer in 2017 producing photography for architects, landscape architects, engineers and interior designers. He also supplies stock images to various clients including the National Trust for Scotland, Conde Nast, the Bank of Scotland and other organisations and publications.

He has won numerous photography awards over the last ten years, including first place in the *Scottish Landscape Photographer of The Year awards* in 2016 and winner of the *British Wildlife Photography awards* 'Urban Wildlife' category in 2018.

"My love of the Hebrides started at a young age when we would go on family holidays to the west coast and over to the islands. I've always been drawn to elemental coastal landscapes and the Hebrides have plenty of those!

Aesthetically, my approach to photography is always to strive for strong, graphic compositions with a desire to simplify the scene into its base elements. I grew up using film and like to get it right in-camera, minimising the amount of time I spend processing images. I do enjoy using long exposures, mainly to simplify water and skies, and create an ethereal atmosphere but aside from long exposures my images are intended to convey a realistic but artistic impression of the landscape.

Understanding the environment is important to me and it plays a big part in my photography. Learning about the geological processes which created it, the natural processes which shaped it or the human history of how the land has been used is all part of my process and helps me to develop a strong connection to place. I'm currently learning Gaelic and even with the little bit I know it has opened my eyes to so much about the landscape of Scotland."

Find out more about Chris and purchase prints at: *www.christopherswan.co.uk*

The dunes of Luskentyre. Fujifilm X–T1, 14mm f/2.8, ISO 200, 8s at f/11. Mar.

ABOUT FotoVUE

fotoVUE's Explore & Discover photo-location and visitor guidebooks guide you to the most beautiful places to visit and photograph.

Contact: mick@fotovue.com
Website: www.fotovue.com

Order at: www.fotovue.com and use code: HEB at checkout to get: 20% off all books

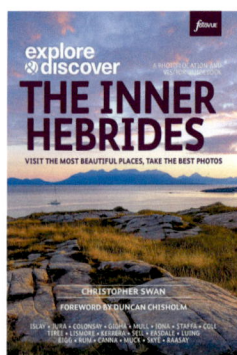
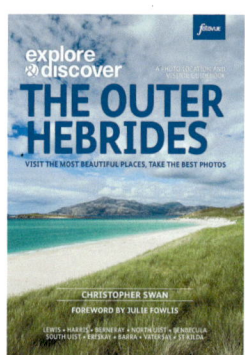
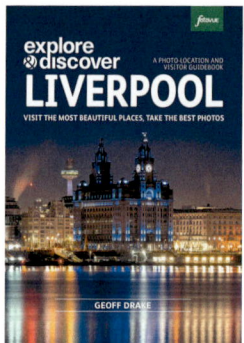
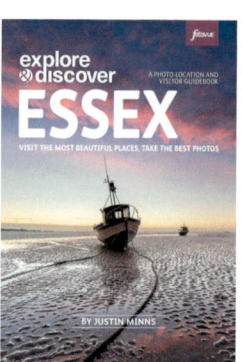

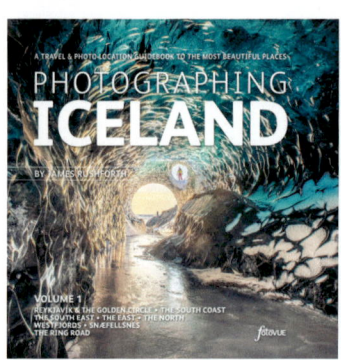

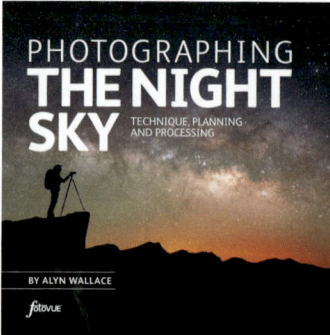

What people say about fotoVUE photo-location and visitor guidebooks

"The best photographer guidebooks by a mile."
"The quality of product is surpassed only by the attention to highly relevant detail."
"This could be the best location-oriented photoguide I have yet to come across."
"A fantastic book and an amazing travel guide."
"The template for all photography location guides."

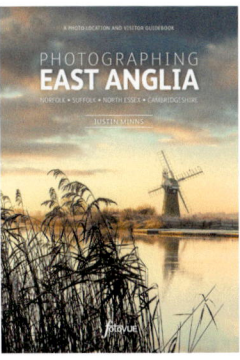
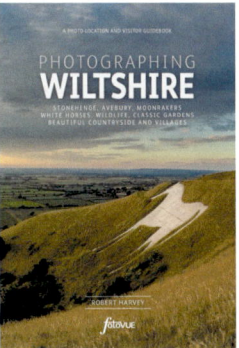

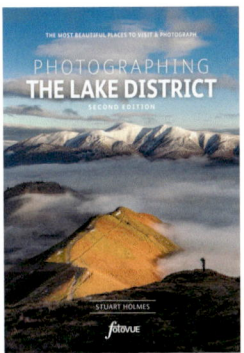
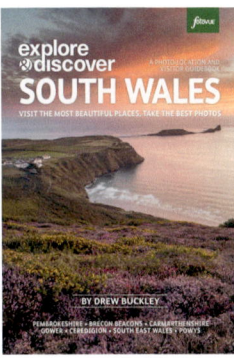
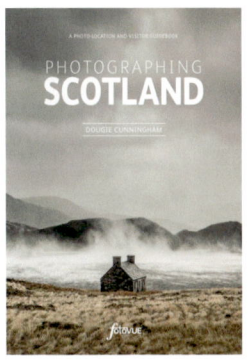
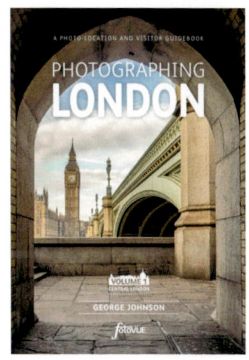

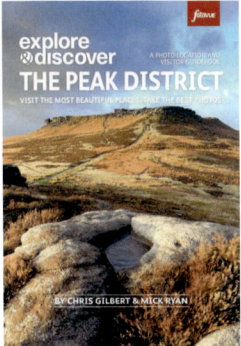

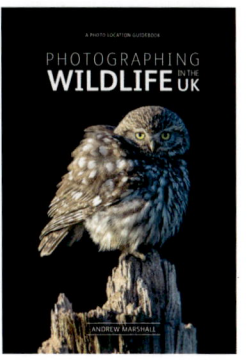

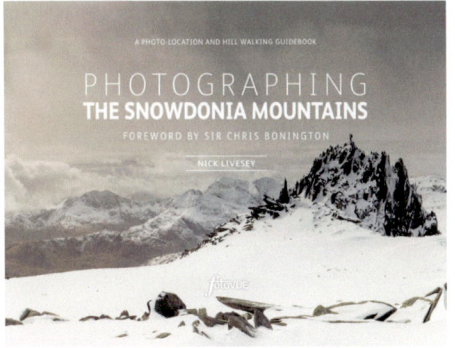

LOCATION INDEX

Borve (Harris) ... 146
Airport, The (Barra) ... 270
Approach from the sea (St Kilda) ... 302
Ardroil ... 96
Atlantic Edge, The (North Uist) ... 206
Bàgh a' Deas ... 292
Bàgh Bhatarsaigh ... 291
Bàgh Halaman ... 264
Bàgh Steinigidh ... 148
Balranald ... 212
Barpa Langass ... 214

BARRA ... 258
Beaches, The (South Uist) ... 232
Beaches, The (Vatersay) ... 288

BENBECULA ... 220
Bernera Bridge, The ... 86

BERNERAY ... 186
Bhaltos Peninsula, The ... 92
Borve ... 148
Borve beach ... 152
Borve to Scarasta ... 148
Bosta Beach ... 88
Breivig ... 278
Butt of Lewis ... 65
Callanish ... 78
Callanish I ... 78
Callanish II ... 84
Callanish VIII ... 86
Carnish Peninsula ... 101
Castlebay ... 260
Castlebay and Heabhal ... 260
Ceapabhal ... 156
Cleat ... 269
Cliff Beach ... 92
Conachair ... 310
Crannag ... 276
Cùl-Phort ... 238
Culla ... 226
Dail Beag ... 70
Dail Mòr ... 68
Dail Mòr, Dail Beag and Stac a' Phris ... 68
Dùn ... 312

Dùn and Ruabhal ... 312
Dun Carloway ... 77
Earsary ... 278
East Beach ... 192
East Beach, The (Berneray) ... 192
East coast, The (Barra) ... 278
Eilean Glas Lighthouse ... 176
Eoligarry ... 275
Eòrasdail ... 294
Eoropie Beach ... 66

ERISKAY ... 246
Finsbay to the North ... 168
Gables, The (Vatersay) ... 286
Gap and Conachair, The ... 310
Gap, The ... 310
Garry ... 56
Geàrraidh an Mònadh ... 237
Gearrannan Blackhouse Village ... 74
Golden Road, the ... 164
Great Bernera ... 86

HARRIS ... 112
Heabhal ... 262
Howmore ... 232
Hùisinis ... 170
Kisimul Castle ... 260

LEWIS ... 54
Loch Bi ... 240
Loch Sgioport ... 240
Lochs and mountains (South Uist) ... 240
Losgaintir, Road to ... 116
Luskentyre ... 116
Main Street, St Kilda ... 306
Mangersta ... 102
Mangersta Beach ... 102
Mangersta Stacks ... 106
Macleod's Stone ... 142
Nisabost ... 130, 138
North Barra ... 270
North Harris ... 170

NORTH UIST ... 196
Northern Coast, The (North Uist) ... 200

Location	Page
Northernmost Point, The (Lewis)	62
Northton	156
Northton and Ceapabhal	156
Northton Salt Marsh	156
Our Lady of Sorrows	237
OUTER HEBRIDES FAR SOUTH	**252**
OUTER HEBRIDES SOUTH	**180**
Poball Fhinn	214
Port of Ness	62
Port Stoth	65
Prince Charlies Beach	248
Reef Beach	94
Rodel	164
Rodel and the Golden Road	164
Rodel to Finsbay	166
RSPB Loch Druidibeag	240
Ruabhal, Benbecula	222
Ruabhal, St Kilda	312
Scalpay	176
Scarasta	148
Scolpaigh Tower	206
Seilebost	130
Seilebost and Nisabost	130
Seilebost Beach	130
Seilebost Viewpoint	134
SOUTH UIST	**230**
ST KILDA	**298**
St Kilda view (North Uist)	208
Stac a' Phris	68, 72
Teampull na Trionaid	214
Tobha Mor	232
Tolsta	56
Tràigh Bhàlaigh	205
Tràigh Eais	272
Tràigh Ear	202
Tràigh Ghearadha Stacks	60
Tràigh Hamara	267
Tràigh Hòrnais	200
Tràigh Iar (Harris)	142
Tràigh Iar (North Uist)	202
Tràigh Iar (Berneray))	188
Tràigh Iar and Macleod's Stone	142
Tràigh Lingeigh	200
Tràigh Mheilein	172
Tràigh Mhor (Lewis)	56
Tràigh Mhòr (Harris)	152
Tràigh Rosamol	120
Tràigh Rosamol Dunes	125
Traigh Siar	291
Tràigh Stir	208
Tràigh Tuath	267
Tràigh Udal	202
Uig	96
VATERSAY	**284**
Village , The (Eriskay)	250
Village and Broch (Lewis)	74
Village bay (St Kilda)	304
Village, The (Eriskay)	250
Virgin Mary and Child statue (Barra)	262
West Coast, The (Barra)	264